# Florida Real Estate Exam Prep 2020 – 2021

***Complete Review with 400 Questions and Detailed Answer Explanations for Licensing (2 Tests for Sales Associates and 2 for Brokers)***

# Table of Contents

# Disclaimer

This guide and all of its chapters are meant for study purposes. The laws mentioned in this guide are for informational purposes only. This guide does not provide legal advice in any way, shape or form. Please refer to qualified and registered lawyers in your state for legal advice.

# Introduction

Whether you're buying or renting in a personal or professional capacity, or you have properties you would prefer to have managed professionally, chances are you will need a realtor. Real estate sales associates and brokers play a crucial role in helping people to find what they're looking for and they also facilitate the rental or purchases of properties.

Becoming a Florida real estate sales associate or broker is a challenge you have decided to undertake. There are local and federal codes and laws you will have to know, as well as paperwork, forms, procedures and so on that you need to understand in order to do the job correctly.

In this study guide, you will find:

- Florida's pre-qualification requirements for the sales associate real estate exam
- Florida's pre-qualification requirements for the broker real estate exam
- How to register for the sales associate and broker real estate exams
- Registration fees
- The process for completing your electronic fingerprinting, locations and costs
- The process of rescheduling or canceling your exam
- The format and rules for the exam
- How to apply for special testing accommodations if you need them
- Things to expect on testing day
- An overview of what will be covered on the sales associate exam
- Things to know for your Florida Real Estate Sales Associate Exam
- Things to know for your Florida Real Estate Broker Exam
- Two practice tests and answers with explanations for the sales associate exam
- Two practice tests and answers with explanations for the broker exam

# Chapter 1: Pre-Licensing Requirements

There are three basic requirements that you must meet before you can become a real estate sales associate or broker. You must:

- Be at least 18 years old
- Have a valid social security number
- Have a high school diploma or GED

In addition to these requirements, there are pre-licensing requirements that each sales associate and broker must also meet before being allowed to take the state exam. Those pre-licensing requirements are different for sales associate and brokers. Below, we will discuss these differences.

Pre-licensing courses vary in length. Online courses allow you to set your own pace, while classroom courses can last from a few weeks to a few months depending on which real estate license you are applying for. Broker courses will most likely take longer than sales associate courses since more course hours are required for brokers.

Additionally, online courses can usually be started immediately, while in-person classroom courses generally have a scheduled start date, scheduled class times and a set end date. To accommodate people, many schools and programs offer a variety of times for in-class pre-licensing courses to allow you to find the one that best fits your schedule.

Online courses are not for everyone. Keep in mind that it will be your responsibility to manage your time and complete the work. You will need to have access to a computer and internet in order to take the online courses as well. An online course is not ideal for those who are not self-starters or who need the support of a teacher along the way. That said, many online programs do allow you to email or IM professors for support.

## Sales Associate Pre-Licensing Requirements

Before taking your Florida Real Estate Exam, you will be required to take a pre-licensing course, have your electronic fingerprints taken as part of your background check and successfully pass the exam at the end of your pre-licensing course.

Approved by Florida R/E commission

Florida offers pre-licensing courses for sales associates in two settings. Choose whether a classroom setting or an online course is best for you, and be sure that the course you choose is state-approved. If you're not sure where to look, most real estate schools and real estate associations across the state offer pre-licensing courses.

The pre-licensing course required for sales associates is 63 hours. Course packages generally range between $60 and $360 depending on the course, school and setting. The pre-licensing course will cover:

- Real estate laws
- Real estate principles and practices
- Real estate math

The time you spend in your course is very important. Florida requires your pre-licensing course hours to be monitored closely. If the minimum 63 hours are not met, the instructors/institution will not be allowed to give you credit.

To ensure you get full credit for your pre-licensing course, be sure to get all the required class hours in. For online courses, be sure to enter the video lecture on time and do not log out until it is through. For classroom courses, be sure to arrive before the class begins and do not leave until the class concludes.

In order to pass the course and receive your certification of course completion, you must pass the exam at the end of the pre-licensing course with a 75% or higher.

The certification of completion that you receive after passing the pre-licensing exam will be valid for two years. This means that you do *not* have to repeat the 63-hour pre-licensing course so long as you take and pass your state real estate exam before the two-year mark. If you fail to obtain your Florida Real Estate Sales Associate License before two years pass, you will be required to pay for and complete the pre-licensing course all over again.

## Exceptions to the Pre-Licensing Course Requirements

Florida makes three exceptions to the pre-licensing course. Those exceptions are as follows:

1. If you are legally licensed to practice law (meaning your license is up-to-date and valid) in the State of Florida, then, you are *not* required to complete and pass a real estate pre-licensing course. Instead, you may complete your application and register to take the Florida Real Estate Exam by attaching a copy of your current Florida Bar credentials to the exam application.

2. You have attended an accredited real estate school, technical center, community college or university, successfully received your credentials showing you've passed the course and the real estate course or courses meet the following requirements:
   - Covers the required course materials of a pre-licensing course
   - Is 63 hours or more
   - Meets the real estate commission standards

   Then you may attach your transcripts or certification from your educational institution to your application.

3. You have successfully graduated with a bachelor's degree or higher in the field of real estate, from a university or institute of higher learning that meets the Florida Real Estate Commission's guidelines for coursework. You may then attach your official transcripts to your real estate exam application.

*NOTE: The Florida Real Estate Commission may require you to submit other supporting documents before it approves your credentials and application for the exam.*

## Requirements Specific to Brokers

A real estate sales associate is an entry-level real estate position. If you enjoy your career and are striving to branch out, then your next step is most likely to become a real estate broker. To take this next step in your real estate career, there are four basic requirements you need to meet first.

The first three basic requirements are the same as those for a real estate sales associate. You must:

- Be at least 18 years old
- Have a valid social security number
- Have a high school diploma or GED

Additionally, in order to become a real estate broker, you must also work as an active real estate sales associate for at least two years over a five-year period.

In addition to meeting these four basic requirements, any real estate sales associate wishing to become a broker must also complete a pre-licensing course.

## Broker Pre-Licensing Requirements

Before taking your Florida Real Estate Exam, you will be required to take a pre-licensing course, have your electronic fingerprints taken as part of your background check and successfully pass the exam at the end of your pre-licensing course.

Florida offers pre-licensing courses for real estate brokers in two settings. Choose whether a classroom setting or an online course is best for you, and be sure that the course you choose is state-approved. If you're not sure where to look, most real estate schools and real estate associations across the state offer pre-licensing courses.

The pre-licensing course required for real estate broker is 72 hours long. Course packages generally range between $150 and $400 depending on the course and setting you choose. The pre-licensing course will cover:

- Real estate brokerage
- Values, listing and selling of properties
- Contracts, financing and financial aspects of real estate
- Environment, zoning and planning as it relates to real estate
- Property management and the real estate market

In order to pass the course and receive your certification of course completion, you must pass the exam at the end of the pre-licensing course with a 75% or higher.

The certification of completion that you receive after passing the pre-licensing exam will be valid for two years. This means that you do not have to repeat the 72-hour pre-licensing course so long as you pass your state real estate exam before the two-year mark. If you fail to obtain your Florida Real Estate Broker License before the two years is over, you will be required to pay for and complete the pre-licensing course all over again.

# Chapter 2: Registering for the Exam

After successfully completing your pre-licensing course to become a real estate sales associate or broker, it's time to register for the Florida Real Estate Exam. The application process for the exam has multiple steps and fees. Those steps include:

- Completing an exam application and paying the application fees
- Submitting and paying for digital fingerprinting
- Registering with Pearson VUE (a third-party vendor used by the Florida Real Estate Commission to conduct computerized testing)
- Scheduling your exam
- Paying the exam fee

## Submitting your Application

First you will fill out your real estate exam application and submit it to the Department of Business and Professional Regulations, also known as the DBPR. The application can be found on the Florida Department of Business and Professional Regulations' website: http://www.myfloridalicense.com. Once there:

- Select the "Online Services" tab near the top of the page.
- Click on the "Apply for a License" option.
- Choose the license type. In this case, "Real Estate."
- When you reach the "Getting Started as a Real Estate Professional" page, choose the "Apply for a License" tab.
    - You will then choose either (1) Real Estate Sales Associates, or (2) Real Estate Brokers.
    - Select the application that applies to you. This will most likely be one of the following:
        - Initial Application – Sales Associate License (Form RE1), which is the first option under the Real Estate Sales Associate tab.
        - Initial Application – Broker License – Upgrade from Sales Associate to Broker (Form RE2), which is the third option under the Real Estate Brokers tab.

- This selection will take you to another page. At the bottom of either page, you will be given the option to either
    - Apply Using Online Services
        - This option will take you to a new page. Once there, you will create a log-in profile. Then you will sign into your account and fill out the application as prompted.
    - Apply Using a Printable Application
        - This option will take you to a new page. Here you will find a printable application complete with written instructions. Once printed, you will fill out the application, complete the application checklist and ensure that you have all the required components from the list.
        - Once your application is completed, place it (and all its components, including the fee) in a sealed envelope, and send it to the following address:

Department of Business and Professional Regulations
2601 Blair Stone Road
Tallahassee, FL 32399-0783

Application fees can be paid for using a check or money order. Those applying online can pay with a credit or debit card. Application fees, while subject to change, are currently as follows:

- Florida Real Estate Commission Application for Sales Associate License – $83.75
- Florida Real Estate Commission Application for Broker License – $91.75

## Background Checks and Digital Fingerprints

Florida requires that both sales associates and brokers pass a local, state and federal background check before their application for the exam is approved. As part of this background check, all applicants are required to submit digital fingerprints.

In addition to the information provided below, the Florida Department of Business and Professional Regulation's website offers a PDF document,

"Frequently Asked Questions – Electronic Fingerprinting,":
http://www.myfloridalicense.com/dbpr/servop/testing/documents/finger_faq.pdf.

This document gives you details on the digital fingerprinting requirements and what you need to bring with you. One of the details you will find on this information sheet will be the Originating Agency Identification Number, commonly referred to as the ORI number.

The ORI number will inform the Florida Department of Law Enforcement of why you need the background check and which agency they need to send your background check results to. For the purpose of Florida Real Estate Agents and brokers, your ORI number is FL920010Z. This is the number you will need when filling out your background check information. The wrong ORI will result in your background check not being completed.

The DBPR accepts digital fingerprints from any Live Scan Service Provider that is Florida Department of Law Enforcement-approved. A list of approved Live Scan service providers can be found by going to the Florida Department of Law Enforcement website at http://www.fdle.state.fl.us/. The following steps will take you to the current approved list of Live Scan vendors in Florida:

1. Choose the "Quick Links" tab at the top of the webpage.
2. On the "Quick Links" page, you will find the link for Live Scan Service Providers in the list under the "Criminal Justice Information" heading.
3. Click the link which will take you to the "Obtaining Criminal History Information" page.
4. Near the bottom of the page, you will find the link for the "Current list of Live Scan Providers."
5. Click the link.
6. This will pull up the FDLE printable list of current approved Live Scan vendors and their contact information.
    a. This will allow you to choose the one that is most convenient for you and arrange to have your digital fingerprints taken.

Once you have chosen a Live Scan vendor, you will need to schedule an appointment, as walk-ins are not allowed. Depending on the vendor you have chosen, appointments can be made online or by phone. Vendor phone numbers will be listed on the Florida Department of Law Enforcement's website.

When you make your appointment with the Live Scan vendor, you will be given an appointment confirmation number. You will be required to provide this as part of your identification verification when you arrive for your appointment.

Real estate sales associates and brokers are required to complete a Level 2 background check, which will be performed by the Florida Department of Law Enforcement. A Level 2 background check includes local and state background checks, as well as an FBI background check. The check includes fingerprinting.

Fingerprinting should be done a minimum of five days before you submit your licensing exam application. Failure to have your fingerprinting completed before your application is processed will cause your application to be flagged and rejected, and you will be required to resubmit the application and go through the process again.

As part of the digital fingerprinting process you will be asked to fill out your demographic information. This information must be accurate and complete, or your background check will be declined.

The demographic information you will be asked to provide for your background check includes:

- Full name
- Maiden name or aliases (if you have either)
- The country in which you are a citizen
- Social security number
- The city and state in which you were born
- Gender and race
- Height and weight
- Eye and hair colors
- Home *and* work addresses
- Home phone number
- Email address

In addition to providing your demographic information you will be required to show two valid forms of ID when you arrive for your appointment. This will include a primary and secondary form of identification. The identification you provide *must* match. Your number-one form of identification *must* be a government-issued photo ID. Primary identifications that are accepted by Live Scan vendors include:

State-Issued Identification:

- Driver's license
- Identification card

U.S. Government-Issued Identification:

- U.S. passport
- Military ID
- DOD Common Access Card
- U.S. work visa with photo

Foreign Government-Issued Identification:

- Foreign passport
- Foreign driver's license

Secondary forms of identifications that are accepted by Live Scan vendors include, but are not limited to:

- Pay stubs
- Bank statements
- Credit or debit cards
- Marriage license
- Birth certificate
- Social security card
- School photo ID
- Vehicle registration
- Voter registration card
- Citizenship or naturalization certificate

The name, address, birthday and any other pertinent information on both forms of ID *must* match, as well as match the demographic information you provided. You will *not* be allowed to complete your digital fingerprinting if the required information and identification are not provided or your identification does not have matching information.

## Fingerprinting and Fingerprints

The cost of Live Scan digital fingerprinting can vary from vendor to vendor, and it also varies based on your licensing profession. On average, digital fingerprinting will cost between $40 and $90.

The Florida Department of Law Enforcement will keep your information on file for six months from the day you have your fingerprints taken. You should ensure that your exam application is submitted and approved before that six-month period is over to ensure that if there is a problem with your application you have time to correct it and provide any required documents. If your application is not approved before the six months is up, you may be required to resubmit your application, including your digital fingerprinting and background check.

Fingerprinting take as little as five to ten minutes to complete and your results are usually received by the Department of Business and Professional Regulations within two to four days. Your fingerprints will be valid with the DBPR for 12 months from the date the FDLE receives them. Once received it can take from 10 to 30 days to have your application and fingerprints approved.

*NOTE: If your fingerprints show that you have a criminal history, your application will be flagged for review. The department will review your criminal history thoroughly to decide if your past crimes will disqualify you from obtaining a license in the profession of your choosing. You will be notified if your application needs to be reviewed by the board or if you will be required to appear in person, before any further measures can be taken regarding your application.*

# Chapter 3: Registering with Pearson VUE

When your background check has cleared, your application will be processed, and you will be notified, by Pearson VUE that your application has been accepted and approved. Once your application has been approved, you will then be able to register for your Florida Real Estate Licensing Exam.

Florida's Department of Business and Professional Regulations uses Pearson VUE to conduct all its professional state testing. The exam you take through Pearson VUE will be a computer-based test that is taken on a small touchscreen computer.

Pearson VUE will receive notice once your exam application has been approved. Once that approval is received, Pearson VUE will send you an official letter informing you of your eligibility to register for the exam.

Pearson VUE has 21 testing sites in Florida. They also offer testing at their facilities Monday through Saturday to accommodate everyone's schedules as much as possible. Choose a date and time that work best for you. Then choose one of the Pearson VUE testing sites that is most convenient for you:

1. Boynton Beach
2. Coral Gables
3. Doral
4. Fort Lauderdale II
5. Fort Myers I
6. Fort Myers II
7. Gainesville
8. Hollywood
9. Jacksonville
10. Lakeland
11. Lake Mary
12. Melbourne
13. Miami
14. Orlando
15. Oakland Park
16. Ormand Beach

17. Pensacola
18. Sarasota
19. St. Petersburg
20. Tallahassee
21. Tampa

## Making your Exam Reservation with Pearson VUE

To make your exam reservation with Pearson VUE, you may call or make a reservation online. To make your reservation you can:

- Call:
  - (800) 204-6289 to reach Pearson VUE Customer Care. Calls are accepted weekdays from 8:00 a.m. to 11:00 p.m. EST. Customer care also takes weekend calls on Saturdays from 8:00 a.m. to 5:00 p.m. EST, and Sundays from 10:00 a.m. to 4:00 p.m. EST.
  - Reservations can be made by phone until the day of testing, so long as they are made before the exam begins.
- Online:
  - http://www.pearsonvue.com
  - Select the "For Test Takers" tab at the top of the webpage.
  - Then click on the "Schedule an Exam" link, which will take you to the "Start Here: Select Your Program" page.
  - Select the "Florida Real Estate and Appraisers" link.
  - On the Florida Real Estate page, you can choose to Create an Account or Sign In on the right side of the web page.
  - Once signed in you will be able to choose the available date and time that works best for you to take the exam. ***This page will also offer you additional exam information.*

Pearson VUE does *not* allow walk-ins. All appointments must be scheduled before you arrive for testing. Testing centers are closed on major holidays including New Year's Day, Martin Luther King Jr Day, Memorial Day, Independence Day, Labor Day, Thanksgiving and Christmas.

## Exam Fees

The cost for the real estate exam is $36.75 for both sales associates and brokers. Payment for your exam must be made when you schedule your appointment. You can pay your examination fee by using an electronic check, debit card or credit card. The exam fee is nontransferable and nonrefundable.

If you can't use the payment methods listed, you will need to call Pearson VUE and arrange to pay before the exam. Payments are not accepted at any of the testing centers.

## Rescheduling or Canceling your Exam Reservation

You may reschedule or cancel your exam reservation, without penalty, up to 48 hours before your scheduled exam day. If you do not reschedule or cancel your exam at least 48 hours prior to the scheduled exam day you will be charged for the exam fee.

You will also be charged the exam fee if you are absent on testing day. Absences may be excused if they are a result of illness, a death in the family, etc. Excused absences will require support documents such as a doctor's note.

## Accommodations for Testing

Pearson VUE provides accommodations for those with disabilities. This allows Pearson VUE to make reasonable accommodations for those with documented disabilities who need the accommodations in order to take their exam.

There are no standardized accommodations. The accommodations that can be provided to you are specific to your personal needs. The testing accommodations that are offered to examinees through Pearson VUE include things like:

- Separate testing rooms
- Extra time to take your exam
- A person or computer program that will read the exam to you

Accommodations are determined by the functional limitations of the examinee. Your disability and functional limitations will need to be clearly stated in the documents you submit when requesting accommodations. Documentation may need to include a written statement from your diagnostic physicians.

# Chapter 4: Exam Day – What to Expect

On the day of your exam, you should wear clothes that are business casual and comfortable enough to sit in throughout the examination. Be sure to wear something that is comfortable in case you find the testing room warm, and a sweater or jacket in case the room is cool.

You are required to arrive 30 minutes before your appointment time to check in for your exam. You will need to bring the following items:

- Two forms of ID, one of which *must* be a government-issued photo ID
- Florida Real Estate Authorization Notice
- One of the three following items:
    - Certificate of pre-licensing course completion
    - Florida Bar card
    - Letter of Education Equivalency from the DBPR

Upon arriving, you will check-in. This will include:

- Confirming your appointment time
- Reviewing your documents and verifying your identity
- Taking a picture for your Pearson VUE profile and Score Report
- Reviewing the "Pearson VUE Candidate Rules Agreement." A copy of the agreement can be found on the Pearson VUE webpage at https://home.pearsonvue.com/candidate-rules-agreement
- Signing electronically for the exam
- Obtaining a locker and key for any personal items that are not allowed in the testing room

Personal items not allowed in the testing room include, but are not limited to:

- Cell phones
- Bluetooth headphones or earbuds
- Any PDAs, tablets or other electronic devices
- Purses, briefcases, backpacks, etc.
- Books
- Paper
- Writing utensils

- Food and drinks

The above-mentioned items and any other personal items should be left in the locker provided, or they should not be brought into the testing center. Pearson VUE clearly states that the company, center, employees and anyone else associated with the company is not liable for anything stolen, lost, damaged, etc.

Once check-in is complete, examinees will be asked to either sit in the lobby until it's time to go into the exam room, or be taken directly to the testing room. If you are asked to wait in the lobby, a test administrator will come get you at your testing time or when a workstation becomes available.

Once you are in the testing room, a test administrator will assign you to a workstation. Pearson VUE testing workstations are equipped with a computer, mouse and keyboard. The test administrator will log you onto the computer. You will not be provided with any other testing materials, such as pencils, paper or calculators.

The computer will offer you a tutorial to show you how to navigate through the exam. A period of up to 15 minutes will be allotted for you to view the tutorial and understand how to navigate your exam. You will also be allowed to ask the test administrator questions, if you have any at this time.

Test administrators are ONLY allowed to answer questions that relate to the computer, program or any other procedure-based questions. They are not allowed to answer any questions about the actual exam.

The 15 minutes you are given to familiarize yourself with the computer format is NOT part of your three-and-a-half-hour testing time. Once you have a feel for the computer and how to navigate it, you will be allowed to start your exam. Because the exam is computerized, your time will begin as soon as you open the first question.

*NOTE: If English is your second language, you may also bring with you an English dictionary.*

## What if you arrive late?

If you arrive at the testing center before the scheduled test time, but after the 30-minute check-in time, you will still be allowed to check in without penalty. If you arrive after your scheduled exam appointment time, the testing facility manager will determine whether you can be worked into that day's testing schedule.

If you are late because of an emergency and have documentation to prove why, you will either be worked into the schedule or your exam will be rescheduled at no additional fee.

If you do not have a valid reason for being late, it will be considered "unexcused." In the event that you have an unexcused tardy, and the testing center cannot work you into that day's schedule, you will be made to reschedule your exam, asked to pay the $36.75 fee for the new exam and marked as a "no show" for the day you were tardy.

## Exam Format

Sales associates and brokers in the State of Florida are given 100 multiple choice questions on their computer-administered test.

Examinees for both the sales associate and broker exams will be given three and a half hours to complete their exam.

The Real Estate License Exam for Sales Associates is composed of:

- 45 questions on Florida real estate principles and practices
- 45 questions on Florida and federal government laws
- 10 questions on real estate math

The real estate license exam for brokers is composed of:

- Florida real estate principles and law, which includes:
    - Real estate brokerage
    - Valuing, listing and selling property
    - Contracts, financing and closings
    - Federal income tax laws

- Investment and the real estate market
- Environmental issues
- Zoning and planning
- Property management

When you are finished with the exam, signal the testing administrator, and wait to be excused before you leave the testing room.

## Exam Scoring and Test Results

Once the exam is complete, examinees will receive their scores immediately. Score requirements for the sales associate and broker exams are the same. You must score a minimum of 75 out of 100 to pass the exam.

When you have completed your exam, the score report will immediately be generated for each examinee. The photo that was taken when you checked in will appear on your score report. In addition to your picture and scoring, the score report will also have instructions to tell you what steps you need to take next.

Check over your score report before leaving the testing center. Ensure that your personal information is all correct. If any changes need to be made, inform Pearson VUE staff before leaving the facility, and ensure you get a copy of the score report after the appropriate changes have been made.

Pearson VUE will ensure that your scores are sent to the Florida Division of Real Estate and/or the Florida Department of Business and Professional Regulations after testing is complete.

If you do not pass the real estate exam, you must wait at least 24 hours before you will be allowed to make reservations to test again. The State of Florida allows you to retake the exam as many times as you need in order to pass. You will be charged the exam fee of $36.75 each time you take the exam.

# Chapter 5: Exam Content

There are different exams for sales associates and brokers. In part, this is because a broker has more responsibility and liability than a sales associate. While the exams will be different and cover some different materials, they are the same in that they each have 100 multiple-choice questions per exam.

This section will review the information you will need to know for your exams.

## Sales Associates

The real estate sales associate exam will have questions regarding any of the following content:

- The business of real estate
- Laws and qualifications for licensing
- License laws
- Real estate commission guidelines and rules
- Activities and procedures
- Violations of guidelines, procedure, or laws and the repercussions
- Local, state and federal real estate laws
- Property rights
- Development
- Homeowners associations
- Time-sharing
- Ownership restrictions
- Titles
- Deeds
- Legal terms
- Real estate contracts
- Mortgages for residential properties
- Real estate transactions
- Marketing and analysis as it applies to real estate
- Appraisals in real estate
- Real estate brokerages
- Brokerage opportunities through real estate investment
- Real estate taxes

- Real estate planning
- Real estate zoning

The above-mentioned topics are all things covered in your sales associate pre-licensing course. We will also touch on them again here in this study guide.

## Brokers

The real estate broker exam will have questions regarding any of the following content:

- The business of real estate brokerage
- Valuing properties
- Listing properties
- Selling properties
- Real estate marketing
- Real estate contracts
- Financing for real estate purchases
- Closings
- Federal tax laws
- Investments
- Zoning
- Planning
- Real estate as it pertains to environmental issues
- Property management in real estate

The above-mentioned topics are all things covered in your broker pre-licensing course. We will also touch on them again here in this study guide.

## Key Terms

- **Absentee Owner:** A person who owns property, but doesn't live there. Instead the person usually hires a property manager to handle the everyday care of the property.

- **Abstract of Title:** Compiling the complete history on any given real estate property, including the names of all titleholders and any liens that have been held regarding the property.

- **Acceleration Clause:** A clause that can be found in a loan contract. It means that if a contract is broken, the loan holder or lender may require any balance remaining on the loan to be paid immediately.

- **Ad Valorem:** The value of the property will be used to calculate the total taxes owed.

- **Adjustable Mortgage Rate or ARM:** Interest rates on a loan that can fluctuate higher or lower throughout the life of the loan.

- **Agent:** A person or persons hired to take care of matters on behalf of the person, people or company that hired them.

- **Amortized Mortgage:** A loan in which the principle of the loan and its interest are paid off in full over a set period and on a regular schedule. Those payments will be equal and consistent over the life of the mortgage.

- **Appraisal:** Having a licensed professional view a piece of property, determine the property's overall value as of that date and generate an official report for the appraisal.

- **Appreciation:** The value of a given property, which accrues over time.

- **Arbitration:** When a legal matter is brought before a judge, rather than a jury, a ruling is made regarding the matter, and that ruling is final. By proceeding with arbitration, the parties involved are agreeing to waive further rights to appeal or seek further legal action on the matter.

- **Assemblage:** Multiple properties which share property lines and are both owned by the same person or entity.

Tax

- **Appraised Value:** Each county assesses the property contained within its county lines. That value is what the county uses to determine the property taxes owed on any given property.

Loan

- **Assumption:** Occurs when an established mortgage belonging to one person or entity is taken over by another person or entity.

Loan

- **Balloon Payment:** A payment made on a loan that is much higher than the usual monthly payment.

- **Basis:** The total of a property's purchase price, closing costs and any additional improvement or concession costs added together.

  purchase price + closing costs + improvements + concessions =

- **Benchmark:** A permanent marker that is installed by official surveying. It measures sea level.

- **Bilateral Contract:** A contract entered upon through a mutual agreement.

- **Biweekly Mortgage:** Payments made on a mortgage that are paid every two weeks or every 14 days.

- **Blanket Mortgage:** Often used in purchases made by developers, though it can be used in other cases. The mortgage is used when multiple properties are purchased together.

Marketing

- **Blind Advertisement:** A property that doesn't have a brokerage firm listed with it. Instead, information including address or P.O. box and a phone number is provided in the advertisement.

- **Blockbusting:** An illegal practice in which someone, using fear, coerces a property owner into selling at a less than fair market value, and then resells that same property for a much higher price in order to make a lucrative profit.

- **Broker:** An individual licensed to conduct business relating to the purchase, sale and other business ventures pertaining to any real estate in Florida.

- **Broker Associate:** An associate who works under a broker but is also qualified in the State of Florida to be licensed as a broker in his/her own right.

- **Buffer Zone:** Land that separates other properties, such as an acre lot between a subdivision and a strip mall.

- **Building Code:** Local governments set specific material and construction guidelines that are standardized throughout the field. This is done to ensure that all construction of new properties, as well as improvements or changes to older properties, is done safely by standardizing operations and some of the materials used.

- **Building Inspection:** Each city or county has a person or department that handles building inspections. An inspection by said individuals is required on every new property before people can occupy the space. These inspections ensure that both residential and commercial properties are built to at least the minimum standardized building codes to ensure everyone's safety, and the structural integrity of the building.
- **Building Permit:** Written permission from the city or county that is required for new construction to begin, or for the remodeling, repairing or demolition of existing residential and commercial buildings.

- **Buyer's Marker:** When the real estate market is saturated with significantly more inventory than there is a demand to buy those properties.

- **Capital Gain:** When your investment or real estate property grows in value and the property values become higher than the price at which you purchased it.

- **Cash Flow:** The final result of the yearly net income minus closing costs, debts, liabilities and various expenses.

- **Certificate of Occupancy:** A document issued by a city or county certifying that a building is safe, and people can now occupy the space.

- **Chain of Title:** The paper trail of a property's owners, in chronological order from the original owner to the current owner.

- **Citation:** Much like a speeding ticket, a citation is issued by the city or county when a minor code or law is broken. A citation often results in the property owner paying a small fee to the city or county for the violation.

- **Commingle:** Refers to personal and professional money being combined.

- **Comparative-Market Analysis (CMA):** When a licensed real estate agent compares the price point at which properties similar to the one he/she is preparing to list. This information is then used to help property owners settle on a fair listing price for their own property.

- **Concurrency:** A system put in place by the State of Florida requiring that any development within the state must first show its ability to grow and thrive should it be allowed to do business.

- **Condominium:** Usually refers to a housing unit that has multiple dwellings within it, each owned by a single individual.

- **Conforming Loan:** A loan that must meet the requirements of the Federal National Mortgage Association (FNMA) and the Federal Home Loan Mortgage Corp.

- **Consent to Transition:** A requirement that must be submitted in writing for a licensed real estate sales associate to transition from being a single agent to a broker.

- **Constructive Notice:** When legal actions are being taken against a person or entity, and the person or entity cannot be reached or served personally, the notice is posted as public record in a newspaper or other public format.

- **Contract:** A legally binding agreement made between two or more individuals or entities. The agreement will outline the terms and conditions of the agreement between the parties, and act as a point of reference in the event that a violation or dispute to the agreement arise.

- **Contract for Deed or Land Contract:** An individual purchasing property by making payments until the purchase price is met. The deed is withheld until the property is paid for in full.

- **Conversion:** When someone uses property or finances that is not theirs without permission.

- **Cooperative:** Created when a body of people come together to mutually support a service or set of services for all those taking part in said cooperative. i.e., an electric cooperative.

- **Corporation:** A business model in which people form a body with the purpose of doing a specific type of business.

- **Cost-Depreciation Approach:** Estimating a property's market value by calculating property purchase cost and adding it to the expense of new building construction on that property.

- **Culpable Negligence:** Neglecting a client or customer to the point that it causes damage to the person on a financial level.

- **Debt:** Refers to any money needing to be paid out by either a payment due or money owed at the end of a set period.

- **Declaration:** The documentation that is compiled when a condominium is formed.

- **Deed:** A document that is given when a property is purchased, showing the ownership of that property.

- **Deed in Lieu of Foreclosure:** Rather than go through the foreclosure process, a property owner may sign over the property deed to a mortgage lender.

- **Deed Restriction:** A condition or conditions placed on a piece of land that all future deed holders must abide by in regard to the property's use.

- **Demand:** The ratio of property available to the number of customers wanting the properties.
- **Depreciation:** When the value of a property decreases for any reason at all.

- **Designated Sales Associate:** A real estate agent who represents both parties in a commercial sale. In order for this style of transaction to occur, a minimum asset requirement of $1 million or more must be held by both the buyer and the seller.

- **Discount Point:** A discount point allows the individual or entity to make a one-time payment at closing. This payment is applied to the mortgage in a bid to lower monthly payment and interest rates on the loan as a whole.

- **Disintermediation:** The withdrawal of money from savings by a depositor that is in turn invested directly with a given borrower.

- **Dual Agent:** A real estate agent that is a representative for both parties during a sale.

- **Due-On-Sale Clause:** A stipulation that may be placed in a mortgage that requires any amount still owed to be paid in full if the property is sold prior to the mortgage being paid off.

- **Earnest Money Deposit:** When renting or buying, earnest money is put down prior to the actual sale and closing, as a commitment to the deal and a show of good faith.

- **Easement:** Allows an individual to use another person's property legally. For example, your home may be behind someone else's property and going through that property is the only way to reach it. So, an easement was part of the contract when you purchased the property, which allows you to use the driveway that cuts from your property, through theirs, and meets the main road.

- **Economic Life:** The length of time in which the value of a property increases from the improvements made.

- **Eminent Domain:** A legal right for private property to be taken by the government and repurposed for public use.

- **Encroachment:** An individual trespassing on a neighboring property.

- **Environmental Impact Statement (EIS):** An analysis of a given area to determine the possible effects building or developing a given area would have on the environment around the site in question.

- **Equity:** The difference between a property's value and the amount still owed on a mortgage.

- **Equity of Redemption:** The opportunity by the mortgage lender to pay off the total debt of a forfeited property, prior to foreclosure, in order to reclaim the property.

Legal

- **Escheat:** A law in each state that grants the state ownership of properties when no will and no relatives are left when someone dies.
- **Escrow:** Money that is held until a decision or transaction is completed.
- **Escrow Account:** An account used to keep funds safe during a transaction.
- **Escrow Account Management:** Agents who hold the funds or assets and manage escrow fees until a time when instructions or a contract fulfillment releases them from that responsibility. This may include money, assets, funds, securities, earnest money, etc.
- **Escrow Disbursement Order:** The legal actions and final determination regarding escrow funds that have been contested.
- **Estate for Years:** A legal written lease that has an agreed-upon duration.

Loan

- **Estoppel Certificate:** The balance due on a mortgage verified in writing.

Loan

- **Exculpatory Clause:** A loan clause that renders the borrower not responsible for the debt personally so he/she cannot be penalized if the loan defaults.
- **Exclusive Agency Listing:** An agreement between a property owner and a broker in which the property owner may find his/her own buyer, therein not owing the broker a commission, in return for not listing a property with any other brokers.
- **Exclusive Right of Sale:** Guarantees a broker's commission even if the property owner secures the buyer.

Tax

- **Exempt Property:** A property that is exempt from paying taxes based on its value.

Legal

- **Familial Status:** A term that defines families with minor children or pregnant mothers.

- **Farm Area:** When a real estate agent chooses to specialize strictly in a set area geographically. This practice allows such agents to learn the area in detail and provide clients with more in-depth details regarding the features that are specific to that location.

- **Federal-Related Transaction:** Loans that, through the federal government, are funded, insured or protected.

- **Fiduciary:** Pertains to an individual who is privileged with ultimate trust.

- **Florida Resident:** A resident that intends to or has lived in Florida for a minimum of four months.

- **Follow-Up:** A practice in which real estate agents touch base with clients shortly after the closing of a sale. Doing so helps to facilitate a professional relationship with clients to encourage them to either use that agent for their next purchase or refer others to them.

- **Formal Complaint:** When the Department of Business and Professional Regulations finds proof of an applicant's misconduct and officially puts those misconducts into an official outline.

- **Freehold Estate:** Ownership of a property by an individual or entity whose length of ownership is indeterminate.

- **Further Assurance:** An agreement in which legal documents for a property are outlined to procure a title free and clear.

- **General Partnership:** Allows both parties to earn or lose profits based on their mutual partnership and shared business.

- **General Warranty Deed:** A guarantee that the real estate is owned free and clear by the seller and he/she is within his/her legal rights to sell the property.

- **Going-Concern Value:** When a property houses a business that is fully functioning and profitable, and that business' value is calculated into the overall property value.

- **Good-Faith Doubt:** A situation that creates the overwhelming impression that a conflict will ensue.

- **Goodwill:** The value placed on a business not by what it owns or the assets it holds but rather by the respectability, loyalty and reputation a business holds.

- **Government Survey System:** A system used by the United States government to mark land developments through land survey lines.

- **Grantee:** The individual or entity that a deed is received by.

- **Granting Claus:** A grantee receiving ownership of property from a grantor.

- **Grantor:** The individual or entity that gives a deed to the grantee.

- **Gross Lease:** A lease that requires a landlord to pay any maintenance or operating costs while the tenant pays a set rent.

- **Gross Rent Multiplier (GRM):** The sale price divided by the monthly rental payments.

- **Ground Lease:** A lease that *only* applies to the property's land.

- **Group License:** Sales associates and brokers receive a license when multiple properties are owned under different names; however, documentation proves that the individual or entity are one-in-the-same or joined through business.

- **Guardian's Deed:** Issued by a judge when the property owner is a minor child, and therefore legally unable to buy or sell property, or when the property owner is deemed mentally unable to make decisions for him/herself and a guardian or power of attorney does so for the person.

- **Handicap Status:** Individuals who, due to physical or mental disability, are significantly restricted in their ability to conduct important everyday tasks, and therefore are protected under state and federal laws.

- **Health Ordinance:** Laws put in place by city and county governments that are designed to protect the well-being and overall health of the citizens that live there.

- **Highest and Best Use:** The real estate practice of using the most lucrative purpose of any given property to determine its worth or value.

- **Home-Equity Loan:** A mortgage, or second mortgage, that is offered by lenders. The value of your home is used as collateral to secure the loan. Therefore, you receive the full loan amount up front and pay back that amount with interest over a five to 15-year period based on the terms of your loan.

- **Homestead Law:** Laws that protect surviving spouses and minor children, as well as any unmarried children of legal age, in the event that the head-of-household or homeowner dies. It allows those individuals to continue living in the home and protects the home from debt collectors or creditors who might impose any kind of lien or confiscate the house for debt repayment. Additionally, the property is also granted a lower real estate or property tax.

- **Household:** A home or dwelling that one or more people live in together.

- **Immune Property:** Real estate properties that are not assessed and which do not pay taxes based on their value. This often applies to local, county, state and federally owned buildings and property.
- **Income-Capitalization Approach:** The rough appraisal value of any given property determined by the anticipated income it will make.

- **Index:** The interest rate of an adjustable mortgage and how it's determined based on the borrower's income and financial position.
- **Installment Sale:** When a property is purchased, and the cost of the property is paid over time through installments.
- **Interest:** A price charged to a borrower by a lender for the use of the lender's money over the period of a loan.
- **Intermediation:** The third party by which borrowers and lenders are connected, such as mutual funds, banks, credit unions and financial advisors.
- **Interpleader:** When money is held by the courts until a time when the judge decides who is legally entitled to the funds.
- **Intestate:** When there is no will for a person who has passed away.
- **Joint Tenancy:** When a property is owned by two or more individuals who are all named on the deed as owners, which allows the property to shift to the remaining owners when one or more of the deed holders dies. For example, this could be a mother and daughter purchasing a home together. When the mother passes away, the daughter becomes full owner of the property.
- **Just Value:** The fair market value placed on a property by an appraiser.
- **Kickback:** A financial gain made by a person or entity for referring business to a specific person or business.
- **Land:** The physical surface of a given property.
- **Leasehold Estate:** A tenant who holds title and ownership of a property that is not actually theirs, but for a period of time it is considered the tenant's own personal property. The four types of leaseholder estates are:

- Estate from period to period
- Estate at sufferance
- Estate and will
- Estate for years.

- **Legal Description:** A legally authorized way of identifying sections of land by their geographical coordinates.

- **Legally Sufficient:** This applies to any statute of Florida laws, Department of Business and Professional Regulations rules or guidelines and/or Florida Real Estate Commission rules or guidelines, and the validity granted to any complaint.

- **Level-Payment Plan:** A plan that allows the borrower to pay the same monthly payment over the life of the mortgage.

- **Leverage:** When real estate is purchased using borrowed capital.

- **Lien:** A legitimate claim by a lender or creditor on an individual's personal property. Usually that property has been used as collateral in securing a loan or credit.

- **Life Estate:** An individual or entity who gains ownership of a given property when the initial owner dies.

- **Lifetime Cap:** The interest rate of an adjustable rate mortgage, and the highest and lowest interest rates that are allowed to be charged over the life of the loan.

- **Like-Kind Exchange:** A transaction in which you sell a property and purchase a similar property. With this exchange a capital gain tax does not occur, and taxes are deferred.

- **Limited Liability Company or LLC:** A business model with corporate structuring that protects the owner's personal assets from company liabilities.

- **Limited Liability Partnership or LLP:** A business model by which the "partners" who own the business have legal protection of their personal assets so that in the event they are sued, there is a limit to the personal assets that can be lost.

- **Limited Representation:** In real estate this refers to a broker who handles the actual transaction of a sale but isn't a part of the listing, showing, buying or selling process in its entirety.

- **Liquidated Damages:** A fee paid by an individual or entity when he/she breaks a contract. For example, when a tenant breaks a lease and moves out before a lease is up. The property owner or manager would then charge the tenant a fee (liquidated damages) for breaking the lease early and costing the property owner or manager the money they would have earned if the person had fulfilled the terms of the lease.

- **Liquidation Analysis:** A way of calculating the minimum value of a property by deducting the property debts from the property's assets, thus resulting in the minimum value the property can hold.

- **Liquidity:** The ability, over the course of a logical time frame, to turn a property's assets into cash.

- **Lis Pendens:** A legal term that refers to being informed of intended legal action.
- **Litigation:** The process of taking legal action regarding an issue, complaint, damages or dispute.

- **Loan-Origination Fee:** A fee that can be added to closing costs by a mortgage company.

- **Loan Servicing:** When a third party collects and processes the payments made by borrowers for any given mortgage company.

- **Loan to Value Ratio:** The ratio of a property's actual value to the loan or mortgage amount.

- **Lot and Block:** A property in a subdivision that contains a single-family home.

- **Market Value:** The most reasonable price at which both the seller and the buyer, with all of the information on the property clearly stated, will sell/purchase a property if neither party is compelled to do so otherwise.

- **Marketable Record Title Act:** Florida Statute, Chapter 712, puts a 30-year limit on title matter defects. Those defects refer to things such as a mortgage, lien, judgment or other such encumbrance that is a matter of public record, which prevent the legal transfer or purchase of a property while such encumbrances allow others to have a claim on the property in question.

- **Meeting of the Minds:** An understanding made between buyers and sellers regarding their intent to enter into a contract with one another and the terms of their agreement.

- **Mediation:** Using the intervention of a non-biased third party to assist in resolving a matter between individuals or parties. This is often used to avoid legal proceedings.
- **Metes and Bounds:** Method of describing a piece of property, regardless of its shape, in a legal and accurate way. The method uses surveying the distance and direction of any given property.

- **Mortgage Insurance Premium (MIP):** A protective insurance paid by lenders to protect them in the event that the borrower should default on a loan.

- **Monument:** A natural or man-made object that marks property boundaries.

- **Mortgage:** The legal contract of terms entered into by a lender and borrower that serves as written proof of a lender's right to sell a given property if the property owner defaults on a loan.

- **Mortgagee:** A lender.

- **Mortgagor:** A borrower.

- **Multiple Licenses:** When, in order to conduct business as part of a brokerage, a broker may be issued more than one license.

- **Negative Amortization:** When the principle balance of a loan increases because the monthly payment or payments are not enough to pay the loan's interest that is accruing.

- **Net Lease:** When a tenant, as part of a lease, pays rent as well as an additional amount that will go towards costs that are usually covered by a landlord.

- **Net Listing:** When a seller and broker agree that any money that is over a set amount earned from the sale of a property will belong to the broker.
- **Nolo Contendre:** A legal term meaning "No Contest," essentially rendering a person or entity guilty without the actual admittance of guilt.

- **Nonconforming Loan:** Any loan that doesn't meet the standards of the FNMA and FHLMC.

- **Nonconforming Use:** The legal use of a property that is allowed to continue being used for its original intended purpose after the zoning for its location has changed, because the property was maintained before the codes changed.

- **Non-Representation:** Buyers and sellers can choose not to be represented by a real estate broker, but a broker can still work with them to complete the purchase or sale.

- **Note:** A legal document that shows the debt owed, which the State of Florida requires to be included with the documents of a mortgage.

- **Novation:** The ability for either the same persons or different persons to use a new contract in place of an existing one.

- **Open Listing:** When a seller pays a real estate broker a commission if he/she is able to find and secure a buyer for the seller's property.

- **Option:** The right, within a specific time frame, to purchase property under specific terms.

- **Ostensible Partnership:** When two or more people or entities become responsible and liable for the other's actions through their relationship and behavior regarding one another.

- **Over-improvement:** When you make improvements to a property that are of no actual benefit or improvement to that property, and ultimately cost more than any value they might have added.

- **Package Mortgage:** The use of real and personal property to secure a debt.

- **Partially Amortized Mortgage:** A mortgage whose repayment is made with monthly payments of the same value through the end of the loan, which is paid off with a balloon payment as the final installment.

- **Percentage Lease:** When a tenant pays rent on a property and additionally gives the owner a set percentage of any income that the property earns.

- **Periodic Cap:** Refers to an Adjustable Rate Mortgage and limits the length of time and frequency at which an interest rate can be adjusted.

- **Personal Property:** Is not "real" property, but rather property such as cars, ATVs, stocks, bonds, etc.

- **Personal Representatives Deed:** The ability of a person or people who are responsible for an estate after someone dies, to sell the property without the requirement of any assurances about the property they have been put in charge of.

- **PITI:** The Principle (money owed on a mortgage), Interest (an amount charged for the use of the lenders money), Taxes and Insurance which, in combination, make up a mortgage payment.

- **Planned Unit Development (PUD):** The use of land for multiple purposes in a residential area.

- **Plottage:** Property value increased by purchasing multiple properties and joining them together.

- **Point of Contact Information:** This refers to the physical address, mailing address, phone number, email address and any other forms of contact used to reach a real estate broker or sales associate.

- **Police Power:** Refers to laws that are protected by the government concerning the health, welfare and safety of the public as a whole, including laws pertaining to building ordinances and zoning.

- **Pre-closing Inspection:** When a property that is being purchased is inspected before the closing of the sale.

- **Payment Clause:** When a borrower is allowed to make a payment or payments on a mortgage before the due date.

- **Prepayment Penalty:** A clause in some mortgages that charges a penalty fee to borrowers if they pay off their mortgage early.

- **Prima Facie Evidence:** Evidence that is substantial enough that no supporting evidence is needed.

- **Probable Cause:** A legal term meaning the reasonable justification for prosecution.

- **Profit:** The difference between what a property costs and the amount at which it sells for. Any amount over the actual cost is considered profit.

- **Progression:** This is what happens when higher-valued properties move into an area around lower-valued properties, and their presence raises the property value of those lower-valued properties by being in the same locale.
- **Property Management:** Refers to a property that is managed, maintained and operated by a person or company for a third party.

- **Property Report:** A report regarding a property in a subdivision.

- **Proprietary Lease:** A lease being made within a cooperative that is for the use of an individual.

- **Prorate:** When, at the closing of a sale or signing of a lease, the total value of the rent or sale is divided so that the days or months the property isn't owned, or the days in a month that have passed before a tenant signed their lease are deducted from the total to allow a fair price for the portion of the property that was not their own.

- **Public Accommodation:** Properties that are accessed by the general public, such as hotels, motels, community centers, etc.

- **Purchase-Money Mortgage:** An owner-financed (the owner being the seller of the property) mortgage, financing part or all of the purchase price for the buyer. Often utilized when a buyer can't secure a loan through usual channels such as a bank or mortgage company.

- **Quiet Enjoyment:** The promise made by a seller or landlord to a buyer or tenant that there will be no untoward claims on the property and that the buyer or tenant will be permitted to enjoy the property undisturbed.

- **Quitclaim Deed:** A property being deeded to another without the promise of any form of ownership.

- **Real Estate Broker:** An individual that is educated, qualified and licensed in real estate, either of his/her own accord or in representation of another, conducts the commercial selling, purchasing, management, leasing, renting or other miscellaneous acts of real estate.

- **Real Estate Services:** Services offered by a real estate agent including but not limited to the advertising, purchasing, selling, leasing, auctioning and exchanging of real estate.

- **Real Estate:** The property, including lands and their tangible improvements.

- **Real Property:** The acquisition of real estate property and all rights to that property.

- **Recommended Order:** The report produced by a hearing officer, also known as an administrative law judge, pertaining to any and all conclusions or penalties that may apply.

- **Reconciliation:** The final estimated value of a property by an appraiser after he/she has evaluated it.

- **Redlining:** An illegal act, executed by a lender, who refuses to lend to borrowers in a specific locale.

- **Registration:** To be officially placed on the list of recognized individuals and businesses in the State of Florida.

- **Regression:** When a property's value decreases or increases slower than it should because of the properties around it.

- **Remainderman:** When a third party takes ownership of a property when that property's life estate ends.

- **Residential Sale:** Refers to the sale of residential property, parcels of land that are zoned residential or property that is no more than 10 acres and zoned for agriculture.

- **Reverse-Annuity Mortgage:** A loan that sees the borrower receives payments from the lender.

- **Right of Survivorship:** When the interest and property rights are absorbed by the surviving owners of the property through tenancy.

- **Right to Reinstate:** The ability to pull a loan out of default if the borrower is able to pay the delinquent debts.

- **Sales-Comparison Approach:** Using properties located in the same area that are similar to the one you're selling in order to arrive at a reasonable price at which to put your own property on the market.

- **Sales Associate:** A person who is licensed by the State of Florida, who in return for a wage or commission, is employed by a broker.

- **Satisfaction of Mortgage:** When a loan is paid in full and the debt is discharged, the lender will verify that the debt is satisfied by providing written acknowledgment.

- **Seisen:** The documentation showing the title or owner to the property.

- **Seller's Market:** Refers to the real estate market having a high volume of buyers and a low number of properties for sale. This is likely to result in a seller procuring the list price or a higher-than-asked price.

- **Single Agent:** A broker who, during a sale or transaction, represents either the buyer or the seller.

- **Situs:** A property's value which is influenced by the reputation and accessibility it has.

- **Sole Proprietorship:** When a person acts and operates his/her own business.

- **Special Agent:** When a broker, for the purpose of one specific transaction, acts for the interest of the principle.

- **Special Assessment:** A special one-time tax that is placed on a piece of real estate, which benefits directly from public improvements.

- **Special Exception:** When a property is allowed to be used for a purpose that is generally against zoning or other laws.

- **Special Flood Hazard Area:** Refers to any area that has a high likelihood of flooding, specifically at least 1% or more each year.

- **Special Purpose Property:** Properties that do not have a similar comparison property, such as a museum, courthouse or a house of worship.

- **Statute of Fraud:** Laws that require a written contract if they are to be considered enforceable.

- **Statute of Limitations:** A set amount of time in which you can file for legal action to be taken on a matter. After that time you no longer have the option to seek legal recourse.

- **Steering:** A set of local, state and federal laws that bar a sales associate or broker from "steering" buyers of a certain minority toward or away from specific areas.

- **Sub-agency:** When a broker acts in the capacity of a principle, while supervising a sales associate that works under him/her, and the sales associate works in the capacity of an agent to the brokerage.

- **Subdivision Plat Map:** The use of a detailed map that shows the locations and layout of property lots, the roads through the subdivision and any other relevant structures.

- **Subject Property:** The specific property being appraised or otherwise referenced.

- **Subject to Mortgage:** A property that is purchased from one party, wherein that party does not pay off the mortgage on the property upon selling. Rather than getting a new mortgage, the new owners continue making payments on the existing mortgage and allow the remaining amount that is on the existing mortgage to be counted as part of the purchase price by the buyer.

- **Sublease:** When a tenant who is leasing a property moves out while still remaining on the lease, and allows another party to move into the space and pay rent for the duration of the time that they live there, and the original tenant in turn pays the landlord or property manager.

- **Subordination Agreement:** In the event that a borrower become delinquent with multiple debt collectors, a subordination agreement allows a debt collector who had a lesser claim to be put in front of a debt collector with a higher claim through this legally binding agreement.

- **Subpoena:** A legal term that requires an individual to come before an administrative board or judge in a court of law and give an honest accounting as pertains to the hearing in question.

- **Supply:** Refers to the available properties at the time of inquiry.

- **Tax Rate or Millage Rate:** The taxable value of a given property, increased by the tax rate for a specific city, county or state.

- **Tax Shelter:** A lower charge in income taxes, when a set of deductions is eliminated from taxable income, lowering the overall income that is counted to be taxed.

- **Taxable Income:** Any income a person has that is allowed to be taxed.

- **Taxable Value:** Taking the value of a given property, excluding all exemptions, leaving the remainder as a taxable value.

- **Teaser Rate:** Adjustable rate mortgages that are given a special interest rate that is lower than the market's average starting interest rate.

- **Tenancy At Sufferance:** A tenant whose initial property lease ends, but is still allowed to live on the property, per the terms of the original lease, until a landlord arranges to renew the lease or asks the tenant to leave.

- **Tenancy at Will:** This term means that the landlord and tenant do not have a written agreement or lease, and there is no set date to move in or move out of the property.

- **Tenancy by the Entireties:** When a married couple are the only owners of real property.

- **Tenancy in Common:** A property that is co-owned, but the owners have no right to survivorship, and may also have different rights to the property.

- **Term Mortgage:** A type of mortgage that has a balloon payment as the last payment and the borrower is only required to make payments on the loan's interest periodically during the life of the loan.

- **Testate:** When a deceased individual has a will in place before dying.

- **Time-Share:** A single home, unit or property that is either leased or owned by multiple parties, and each owner or tenant is allowed rights to the property for a set duration.

- **Title Insurance:** a type of policy that protects owners and lenders from losses relating to ownership or titles.

- **Title Theory:** The title for a property given to a lender until the borrower has satisfied his/her debt.

- **Toxic Waste:** Any harmful chemical or substance found in water, ground water or soil.

- **Trade Name:** A name used for transactions by a business.

- **Transaction Broker:** A broker that handles the sale and purchase of a property for both parties, and for one side of the parties involved in the transaction.

- **Up Front Mortgage Insurance Premium (UFMIP):** Using a Federal Housing Administration (FHA) loan, and paying the entire cost of a property's insurance premium at closing.

- **Underground Storage Tank:** Usually refers to a container for petroleum-based products such as gas or propane, which is stored underground. The location for the storage tank requires the ground to be dug up, a tank to be placed below the ground and then the container to be completely covered with the exception of an access point.

- **Unenforceable:** When a contract is found to be fraudulent or signed under fraudulent pretenses, then the document cannot legally be enforced, and the contract and its contents become worthless.

- **Unilateral Contract:** A contract where only one of the parties involved is responsible for the fulfillment of its contents.

- **Uniform Standards of Professional Appraisal Practice or USPAP:** Guidelines that every professionally licensed appraiser must follow when conducting an appraisal.

- **Vacancy Rate:** The number of units a property has, that are not occupied, as represented by a percentage.

- **Valid:** When the legal requirements of a contract are met, then a contract is valid.

- **Variable Lease:** A change in rent due after the lease has already begun.

- **Variance:** An exception made, due to hardship, regarding zoning compliance.

- **Void:** Not legally enforceable.

- **Voidable:** A contract that is made with an individual who is a minor or incompetent. These contracts must be upheld by one party, and the minor child or incompetent individual has the right to back out of or break the contract without legal repercussions and cannot be made to honor the terms of the contract.

- **Wrap-Around Mortgage**: When a second mortgage is taken out, and the value of the second mortgage includes the balance on the first mortgage. The borrower will pay a monthly payment to the lender of the second mortgage only, and the lender will in turn pay the monthly payment on the mortgage.

- **Zoning Ordinance:** Refers to city and county laws that dictate the use of property in specific areas such as residential, commercial and industrial.

## Construction and Property Terms

- **Asbestos:** Asbestos is a fire resistant, carcinogenic (cancer-causing) product that is commonly found in older residential homes and commercial properties.

- **Casement:** A window that swings open by its hinges out to one side.

- **Condominiums:** A residential building that contains multiple residential units. Each unit within the building is a single residence. All the units are housed within the same building, each owned or rented by its individual occupants.

- **Corner Lot:** A real property or real parcel of land located on the corner of a given intersection.

- **Dormer:** A roofline that is higher than the main roofline of the home.

- **Double Hung:** Double-hung windows operate by opening vertically from top to bottom.

- **Easement:** An easement, generally made through a legal binding agreement and often written to either be grandfathered into future purchases or contracted to be in all future sales, refers to a property owner's use of a portion of another individual's property which he/she does not own. This generally applies to properties that are located behind another and which can only be accessed through the property that's in front of them.

- **Fixed Window:** A glass window attached as an immovable fixture; it does not open or close.

- **Fixtures:** An item such as a chandelier or mounted toilet paper holder that is permanently attached to a property.
- **Flat Roof:** A roofline equipped with a slight slope for drainage but which is otherwise almost entirely flat.

- **Gable:** A roof with two sloping edges that are completely equal in length and width.

- **Gambrel:** A roofline that has two sloping edges. The edges at the base are more inclined than those at the peak.

- **Roof Ridge:** A roofline that has four sloping sides, known as a hip.

- **Insulation:** A material (which can come in a liquid spray foam that hardens after application, a blown batting in which the insulation is broken down into small pieces, or in rolls) that can be used between flooring, walls and roofing to protect residential, commercial and other structures.

- **Interior Lot:** Any parcel or property that is not located on a corner.

- **Jalousie:** A louver of louvers found in windows or doors, either fixed or adjustable.

- **Key Lot:** A piece of real estate (land, residential property, commercial property, agricultural property, special property, etc.) located in an area which increases the property's value because of its location and/or the properties around it.

- **Land:** The actual, physical surface area of any properties.

- **Mansard:** A roof that has four sides, each with two slopes at different angles and different degrees, with the lower slopes having a much steeper slope than the ones at the top of the roofline.

# Chapter 6: State and Federal Laws

Local government has a profound impact when it comes to real estate. Such government has police powers to enact laws protecting the public's health, safety and overall welfare. Police powers are implemented through zoning laws, building codes and property taxes.

State government plays a different role in real estate. Florida's state laws pertain to protecting the environment and Florida's beautiful waterfront properties through the Department of Environmental Protection (DEP).

Some of the most prominent agencies within the federal government include the Department of Housing and Urban Development (HUD), the Department of Veterans Affairs (VA), the Federal Housing Administration (FHA), and the Federal Reserve system (also known as the fed).

Between local, state and federal agencies there are an array of laws which are created to protect the public, licensed sales associate, broker associate, brokers, the environment and the rights of all parties involved.

The real estate world also has organizations specific to each state that implement rules, guidelines and other such regulations to protect property owners and sales associates, as well as hold those handling real estate matters for the public. Some of those organizations include the National Association of Realtors (NAR), the Florida Association of Realtors (FAR) and local board associations. NAR has a published code of ethics that have been established in order to hold all of its members to a high standard. Those who violate local laws, state laws, federal laws or the bylaws set by these agencies will find themselves meeting harsh punishments that can include temporary or permanent suspension of their license, as well as possible legal ramifications including but not limited to misdemeanors, felonies, substantial fines and jail time.

## Florida State Laws

In this section you will find the current Florida real estate laws. A detailed breakdown of Title 32, Chapter 475 of the Florida statutes, which contains the bulk of laws on sales associate and broker education, codes and discipline can be found below. These laws cover regulations of professions and occupations, education and continued education of real estate associates, and laws pertaining to real estate brokers and sales associates, as well as brokerages. Additionally, you will find other important state laws that are relevant to those working in Florida real estate.

Title 32, Chapter 475, is broken down into various parts. Chapter 475 refers to laws pertaining to real estate brokers, sales associates, appraisers and schooling. That title and chapter is broken down in the following manner:

- **Part I: Subsection 475.001 - 475.5018** pertaining to the schooling, continued education, and rights, responsibilities, and liabilities of sales associates and real estate brokers.
- **Part II: Subsection 475.610 - 475.631** pertains to appraisers.
- **Part III: Subsection 475.700- 475 719** pertains to the commercial real estate sales commission lien act.
- **Part IV: Subsection 470.800- 475.813** pertains to the commercial real estate leasing commission lien act.

Florida has regulated these laws for the well-being of its public, in regard to real estate associates, real estate brokers and their requirements for their education. Under Part I, Chapter 475, Section .001 through .5018 you will find the laws and guidelines relating to sales associates' and brokers' education and general conduct.

**Section 475.02** outlines the requirements and responsibilities of the Florida Real Estate Commission. The commission must have at least seven members, four of which must be licensed brokers. Commission members are appointed to four-year terms. Licensed members of the commission are permitted to teach courses by the Florida Real Estate Commission or the Florida Department of Business and Professional Regulations.

**Section 475.021** outlines the Division of Real Estate and the services provided by it. These services include record-keeping, legal, examinations and investigative services. The Division of Real Estate uses fees and commission assessments for funding and requires that funding only be used for real estate regulation funding.

**Section 475.03** explains the delegation of power for the Florida Real Estate Commission. Members of the commission can make rules and changes by a majority vote, with the exception of disciplinary actions. For those actions they must first have the approval of the attorney general. Additionally, the commission is allowed, for the purposes of advisement on legal matters, to seek the advice of an independent lawyer.

**Section 475.04** pertains to the responsibility of the real estate commission to properly educate professional employees. The commission is responsible for ensuring the proper education of all sales associates, associates, brokers and instructors. This education is required to include business practices, the principles of the real estate business, ethical responsibility and law as it relates to real estate in Florida. Additionally, the commission is also required to facilitate those same individuals with continued education while working and operating in Florida.

The Florida Real Estate Commission may execute its educational responsibilities by approving real estate education courses for all individuals requiring a permit or license through the state. This may include prescribing an educational pathway or forming educational courses. To utilize the resources and cover the costs of the educational programs and materials, the Florida Real Estate Commission may sell a handbook and textbooks that cover any of the pre-licensing education, licensing exam and continued education for students and individuals holding permits or licenses, as well as the public in general. The money earned from these sales will be used by the real estate commission to meet its financial obligations. The State of Florida will own the copyright to all educational material released by the Florida Real Estate Commission or the Department of Business and Professional Regulations.

**Section 475.045** pertains to the Florida Real Estate Commission Education and Research Foundation. The purpose and responsibilities of this foundation include educational expansion for those seeking to be licensed or who are already licensed in the State of Florida. The foundation is also responsible for the improvements of current real estate programs, the instructors who teach them and degree programs in colleges and universities in the field of real estate.

As part of the education process the Real Estate Commission Education Research Foundation will also do studies throughout Florida pertaining to real estate both directly and indirectly, urban and rural development, and use the result from those findings to improve their educational programs. The educational material used by the Florida Real Estate Commission in the Florida Department of Business and Professional Regulations will be updated regularly to improve the educational courses that are offered in real estate schools, pre-licensing courses, colleges, universities and continuing education programs.

Based on research, the foundation will make suggested changes and recommendations to real estate laws at both a local and state level. Research, conclusions and other relevant real estate information will be published publicly on a periodic basis to provide transparency to the public.

Each year the Florida Real Estate Commission Education Research foundation will make a formal publication to the general public reporting the things it has accomplished that year. By no later than January 1 of any given year, the foundation will report all funds and their uses as well as the foundation's intentions for distributing money for the coming year. In reference to the funds that the foundation holds, the Florida Real Estate Commission can create a proposal and submit it officially to the foundation in order to fund projects.

It is important to know that the Florida Real Estate Commission Education and Research Foundation does not make or distribute educational materials. The information gathered through research is submitted to real estate agents, brokers, real estate schools, colleges and universities. It is then compiled into proposals by those entities and individuals to be submitted to the real estate commission to improve and update its educational content.

**Section 475.05** pertains to the Florida Real Estate Commission's ability to impose bylaws and rules pertaining to real estate education, examination and licensing.

**Section 475.10** pertains to the statute requiring that the commission authenticate its documents and proceedings. To ensure, certify or otherwise identify and acknowledge that proceedings and records are valid and true, certifications of the commission's intentions, wishes and rulings will be marked with the commission's seal.

**Section 475.125** pertains to fees in relation to the Florida Real Estate Commission and the Florida Department of Business and Professional Regulations. Legally, the fees that the real estate commission can apply include application fees, examination fees, reexamination fees, cancelation or rescheduling examination fees, licensing fees, license renewal fees, certifications or re-certification fees, fees for reinstatements of licensing or certification, penalty fees for renewing certifications or licenses late, providing additional copies of certificates or licenses and fees for any record-keeping.

The fees established by the real estate commission are required to generate the finances needed to enforce the requirements and laws that it is legally bound by. To that end, the law stipulates that the original application fee and first examination fee may be no higher than the combined sum of $100. The fee for your initial license and renewing fees may not be higher than $50 each. However, the commission must refund application and/or licensing fees if, after review, the commission determines the State of Florida is not entitled to the fees, or if the commission determines that only a specific portion of the resources offered in the application process have been utilized.

**Section 475.15** pertains to registration and licensing. The commission requires that any form of partnership, company or corporation that operates as a broker in the State of Florida be required to register with the real estate commission and renew their license annually. In the event of a limited partnership then the state only requires that the general partner be a licensed broker or a brokerage corporation. The licensing of a partnership, company or corporation will be canceled if at least one active broker is not legally licensed or registered and the status of his/her license is in force. In the event that the sole broker dies or for any reason suddenly can no longer maintain his/her role, the real estate commission is allowed to install a temporary broker.

**Section 475.161** pertains to the licensing of broker associates and sales associates. In general, a broker associate or sales associate will be licensed as an individual. A license will be issued with a person's legal name alone. Special exceptions can be made if the individual provides documentation from the department of state that he/she is authorized as a professional corporation, limited liability company or professional limited liability company. In the event that a person is licensed as a corporation or company, the law will allow a sales associate or broker associate to be licensed and register as a general partner, member, manager, director or hold other such offices within a brokerage.

**Section 475.17** pertains to the qualifications required to practice as a real estate agent in the State of Florida. The general qualifications include that anyone wishing to work as a licensed real estate agent is required to be a minimum of 18 years old and must have a high school diploma or GED equivalent.

The Department of Business and Professional Regulations and the Florida Real Estate Commission look to license those who have good character. To this end the State of Florida will not license individuals who have been denied a license, disbarred, had a license revoked or suspended, or have committed other offenses that bar them from working in the professional field of real estate in any other U.S. state or territory. These types of situations are taken seriously because as a real estate agent you are handling legally binding contracts and large sums of money.

The State of Florida requires that you successfully complete a number of courses, regulated by the FREC and the DBPR, to ensure that you are properly educated prior to licensing and continue your education to stay current on real estate laws and practices in the future. As detailed earlier in this book, those who wish to become real estate sales associates have specific requirements they must fulfill.

Stricter guidelines are required before a real estate sales associate is permitted to take a broker's exam. The stricter guidelines are designed to ensure that you have the experience, education and understanding of the field before stepping into such a substantial role. As a broker you will be legally responsible and liable for the sales associates that work under you in a brokerage. These guidelines include that you are required to work at least 24 months as a sales associate.

Once you have passed your exam for sales associate or for brokers, you will be required to continue your education as part of your licensing requirements. Forty-five classroom hours of post-licensing education are required before you are allowed to renew your license for the first time. You must complete a post-licensing class exam at the end of the educational course, as well as meet the class hours requirement.

If a real estate sales associate does not complete the required post-licensing education course, fulfill the required course hours and pass the post-licensing education exam before the license is due for renewal, his/her license will be nullified. If this happens, a person will be required to start the process from scratch. Brokers and sales associates will also be required to periodically participate in continued education courses to stay up-to-date on the most relevant real estate laws, practices and taxes.

**Section 475.175** pertains to the laws which dictate the requirements for state licensing examinations. To qualify to take the Florida Real Estate Exam for Sales Associates or Brokers you will be required to complete an application, have digital fingerprints taken and be subjected to a local, state and FBI background check.

The Florida Department of Law Enforcement will process your digital fingerprints and have your information forward to the Federal Bureau of Investigation to ensure that you qualify to take the state licensing exam.

**Section 475.180** pertains to the licensing requirements and qualifications for non-residents of the State of Florida who wish to become licensed as sales associates or brokers within the state. This section also informs licensed Florida residents, who move out of state, that they must inform the real estate commission within 60 days that their residency has changed.

**Section 475.181** pertains to licensure, which requires the State of Florida to license any applicants who have successfully completed their state licensing exam, and not bar those individuals that are qualified. However, the real estate commission is allowed to refuse applicants who have violated any of the provisions in Title 32, Chapter 475 or who have disciplinary infractions.

Applications will expire 24 months or two years after the date in which they were received. State law also prohibits the real estate commission and the Department of Business and Professional Regulations from issuing a license if the applicant is under investigation for violations against his/her licensure.

**Section475.182** pertains to the renewal of licenses and continued education requirements. The Department of Business and Professional Regulations must receive a renewal application and fee in order to renew any license. Renewal applications are only for individuals who are currently sales associates, broker associates or brokers, and whose licenses are currently active. Individuals will need to complete 14 hours of continued real estate education successfully before a renewal application can be approved. Please note that for the first renewal of your real estate license you will be required to complete a post-licensing education course rather than the 14-hour continued education course.

In some cases, a specialty course may be substituted for continued education if the Department of Business and Professional Regulations and the Florida Real Estate Commission approve the course as an acceptable substitute. Additionally, the real estate commission may approve a written examination for a correspondence course or distance learning course as a substitution for continued learning if the appropriate documents are submitted and approved.

If a license is not renewed, the Department of Business and Professional Regulations will automatically mark that license as inactive and will only remove that status if other qualifications are met. Each licensee will receive notice by mail at the last address the DBPR has on file for that individual. For that reason, it is important that you update your personal information with the Florida Real Estate Commission and the Department of Business and Professional Regulations in a timely manner any time that information changes.

**Section 475.182** pertains to a license receiving an active status. An individual can change the status of his/her license to voluntarily inactive. During the time of inactive status, you will still be required to complete 12 hours of continued education courses each year while your license is inactive. State law requires this continued education in order for you to renew your license while it's voluntarily inactive.

When your license has been involuntarily inactive for 12 months or less, you may reactivate your license after you have successfully completed at least 14 hours of commission-prescribed continued education courses. If your license has been involuntarily inactive for less than 24 months but for more than a year you will be required to complete 28 hours of commission-prescribed education courses before it can be reactivated.

Involuntary inactive licenses that have remained inactive for more than two years will expire. If a license expires, it becomes null and void. The Department of

Business and Professional Regulations will inform you 90 days before your license is due to expire. The real estate commission will charge a fee of $100 or less for the late renewal of an involuntary inactive license, along with any other fees that may apply.

The real estate commission may reverse the ruling of a void license in the event that the license renewal was not completed due to a hardship, illness or economic reasons. To have your license reinstated for those reasons, the real estate commission allows six months from the date your license expired for you to renew. Additionally, you'll be required to meet the continued education requirements, pay your licensing fees and ensure that your license is eligible for renewal.

**Section 475.215** pertains to multiple licenses. Brokers may request an additional license. Sales associates and broker associates are not afforded this right, because they are not allowed to be registered with more than one employer at any given time.

In order to be approved to receive additional licenses, proof is required that they are necessary and will not be used in an unlawful way. Multiple licenses may be denied in the event that disciplinary charges have been made, and the broker is in violation of state law. In such instances, not only will the issuance of multiple licenses be denied but a broker's primary license may also be suspended or made void.

**Section 475.22** requires every broker to have a sign in his/her main office, at the entrance. The sign is required to have the name of the broker, and individuals who work in the office. A brokerage partnership or corporation is required to have the name of the brokerage firm, corporation or trade name, along with the name of at least one broker on the sign.

**Section 475.23** pertains to licensure expiring upon a change in address. In the event the broker changes business addresses, the license will no longer be in force. Additionally, real estate schools that operate under a permit, or sales associates working for a broker or instructor of a real estate school will also have their license made inactive in the event that their business address changes.

In order to prevent your license from becoming void or inactive, a change of address needs to be submitted to the real estate commission. When a brokerage or real estate school have a change in business address, they need to notify the commission in writing. Any sales associates or instructors working for the business will need to be mentioned.

**Section 475.24** pertains to branch offices and fees. If a licensed individual wishes to change the business which he/she is working for, the person will be required to notify the real estate commission and the Department of Business and Professional Regulations of the change. Licensed individuals need to be registered through whichever branch office they are working for and conducting business out of. Each office pays a $50 fee annually to maintain their registration with their branch office. Branch offices are required to have at least one broker on staff.

**Section 475.25** pertains to discipline and disciplinary actions. The real estate commission is legally allowed to deny any applicant a registration permit or renewal in the event that a formal complaint has been lodged or disciplinary action is being taken. The licensed individual may be put on probation, have his/her license suspended for up to 10 years and face administrative fines up to $5,000 for each offense committed. A formal reprimand may also be issued in addition to any or all of the above-mentioned items.

If a licensee is guilty of fraud; misrepresenting themselves or someone else; concealing information; making false promises; negotiating under false pretenses; being dishonest by tricking scheming or deceiving; is culpably negligent or in breach of trust in any business dealings in the State of Florida, or any other US state or territory, this will cost the real estate agent his/her license and may also result in criminal charges.

If a licensed agent or client suspects any misconduct by either party, the licensee can defer to the real estate commission and request a review of the issues.

Any illegal acts by a state licensed professional will result in the loss of his/her license and the individual will be barred from holding that license or similar licenses both in the state in which it occurred as well as in the rest of the United States and its territories. Actions will not only be taken by the Florida Real Estate Commission and the Department of Business and Professional Regulations, but actions can also be taken by the Florida Department of Law Enforcement, and if necessary appropriate federal agencies.

Further details pertaining to misconduct or outright illegal actions can be found in Title 32, Chapter 475, Subsection 25.

**Section 475.255** pertains to determining agency and transactional relationships.

**Section 475.2701 thru 475.272** pertains to short title, which cites the "Brokerage Relationship Disclosure Act."

**Section 475.274** pertains to the scope of coverage, authorization of brokerage relationships, brokerage activities and disclosure requirements of residential sales.

**Section 475.2755** pertains to the role, purpose and responsibilities of a designated sales associate. This is further defined in this study guide's key terms, and additional information can be found under Title 32, Chapter 275 of Florida Statute.

**Section 475.278** pertains to authorized relationships as they apply to the brokerage field. This includes brokerage relationships, which can be entered into as either a transaction broker or a single agent. Unless otherwise stated in writing, it should be presumed to be a transaction brokerage.

A transaction broker relationship refers to a broker who represents the buyer, seller or both parties in a limited capacity. These limited capacities require the broker to be fair and honest, account for all funds throughout the transaction and be skilled and diligent throughout the transactions.

Brokers should disclose all relevant facts to the property, present all offers and counteroffers and limit confidentiality. Additionally, brokers assume any mutually agreed-upon duties between everyone involved.

Like a transaction broker, a single agent is loyal, ensures confidentiality, ensures full disclosure, accounts for all funds during the transaction and presents all offers and counteroffers. Unlike a transaction broker, single agents represent either the buyer or the seller, but not both.

**Section 475.28** pertains to the rules of evidence. Rules of evidence pertain to proceedings that can be held before the real estate commission or a civil or criminal court. During these proceedings, payment receipts, expectations and compensations are important items. These are necessary to provide proof of performance of a specific act, service, compensation or other such requirements.

To present such evidence, photocopies can be used when the original document is not available, and accounting and record books can be submitted as proof of business conducted.

**Section 475.28** allows the real estate commission to set up its own rules and guidelines regarding disciplinary actions for violations against rules and guidelines.

**Section 475.31** pertains to final orders in real estate licensing and conduct. In the event that a broker has his/her license suspended or revoked, any sales associates or broker associates working under that broker will find their licenses involuntarily inactive until they are able to find a new employer. The real estate commission is allowed to distribute published final orders or decisions once they become final. It may also publish or withhold at its discretion the name of an address of the broker or brokerage in question.

**Section 475.37** pertains to the reversal of court or commission orders. In the event that a decision made by the courts or the real estate commission is set aside or reversed, the license will be restored, as will any rights and privileges the licensee had prior to the disciplinary action that was taken. Any information used for those proceedings will no longer be able to be held against the licensee.

**Section 475.38** pertains to payments of cost, which deals with commissions fees and end costs, which will not be advanced or executed by any general statute unless the commission is liable for any of the fees or costs.

**Section 475.41** pertains to invalid commissions. It states that any contract for compensation of services is not valid and will not be enforced if the person conducting the service is unlicensed.

**Section 475.42** pertains to violations and penalties as they pertain to real estate and its agents. If an individual does not have a valid license, he/she may not act or operate as a sales associate, broker associate or broker. Anyone who violates this statute is committing a felony of the third degree.

A licensed sales associate may not operate as a broker. Brokers are prohibited from employing an individual as a sales associate if that person does not hold a valid and current license as a sales associate. Real estate sales associates are not allowed to collect money that is related to real estate brokerage transactions regardless of whether it is a commission, deposit, payment, rental or any other monetary payment.

Individuals must comply with any subpoenas. Additionally, they should not obstruct or hinder any lawful activities authorized by the real estate commission or a court of law.

A broker is prohibited from using a trade name unless he/she has properly recorded it with the real estate commission and had it placed on his/her personal license. This section also prohibits knowingly concealing information.

Violations made by anyone in regard to this subsection are guilty of a second-degree misdemeanor and will be punished accordingly. Nothing in this subsection will prevent or prohibit legal action from being taken. In fact, portions of this subsection require that legal action be taken against those who violate it. Depending on the portion of this statute, individuals could find themselves dealing with a civil case or a criminal case, in addition to the denial, revocation or suspension of a license.

**Section 475.43** covers presumptions, which refers to a time when a conclusion is drawn based on assumed facts, logic and reasoning. These things are supported in a court of law and assumed to be accurate and correct, unless definitive proof to the contrary is shown.

**Section 475.451** pertains to schools teaching real estate practices. Every person, school or institute which offers a course of study in real estate practices, does so based on Florida Real Estate Commission precedents regarding teaching, pre-licensing, licensing and renewing of real estate licensing for sales associates and brokers.

There is an exclusive exemption made to career centers, community colleges, colleges and universities.

Anyone wishing to operate a real estate school or be an instructor requires specific qualifications. The school permit holder is responsible for directing and operating the school as a whole. The permit holder is required to be licensed as a broker, and must also pass the state real estate instructors' exam.

To be an instructor you will be required to pass a competency test. You must have a bachelor's degree in a business-related field, its equivalent or a state broker's license; or you can have a bachelor's degree with extensive experience in the field of real estate, and a broker's license. You may also choose to take the instructors' exam approved by the Florida Real Estate Commission.

The real estate commission may require a teaching demonstration or practical exam. The Department of Business and Professional Regulations, upon receipt of a renewal application and application fee, will renew the instructor's permit. Seven hours of continued education will also be required. If an individual fails to renew his/her permit, it will automatically become involuntarily inactive.

Teaching real estate practices without a permit is illegal in Florida. It carries a second-degree misdemeanor for offenders. Additionally, you may not guarantee those taking the course will pass any of the licensing exams or advertise that the course or courses are recommended or endorsed by the REC or DBPR.

As with the sales associate exam and broker exam, a Florida Bar Association card can be provided with the application in place of educational requirements, so long as credentials are in good standing.

All people, schools and institutions are required to keep records for registration, rosters for each course, attendance records, copy of exams and progress tests and student answer sheets for a minimum of three years.

**Section 475.4511** regards the advertising practices of real estate schools. Real estate schools, teachers and other staff members are not allowed to make; arrange for another party to make; approve written, oral, or visual statements, representations, endorsements, or advertisements if they have reason to believe, or know outright, that the information presented is untrue, inaccurate, misleading or otherwise exaggerates information. This applies to all advertising and publicity.

Additionally, school representatives or instructors are not allowed to make guarantees or promises to job applicants, prospective students or the general public in regard to employment or placement in their programs. This includes using over-embellished information to draw prospective students. An actual physical contract is required in order to offer any form of employment.

**Section 475.453** covers rental information including contracts, refunds and penalties. When rental information lists are provided by sales associates or brokers, the list must be current, or any fees for providing the information will legally be required to be returned in full. If you provide rental listings and a prospective tenant doesn't find a place to rent, a portion of that fee may be required to be refunded. Regardless, any fee or portion of fees must be refunded to the prospects within 30 days of the day the sales associate or broker was initially contracted, and an appropriate receipt or contract must note the refund.

The real estate commission has the legal right to determine what is required in these contracts and regarding the business procedures and processes.

Any violation to these guidelines or applicable laws is considered a first-degree misdemeanor. Additionally, a sales associate or broker may have his/her license suspended or revoked by the real estate commission in whatever way the law sees fit.

**Section 475.455** pertains to the exchange of disciplinary information. The real estate commission is required to inform the Division of Florida Condominiums, Timeshares and Mobile Homes, which is a division within the Department of Business and Professional Regulations, of any disciplinary actions that have been taken regarding any sales associate or broker.

**Section 475.482** pertains to the Florida Real Estate Recovery Fund. This fund was created to ensure that any sales associate or broker who has been legally ruled guilty of wrongdoing that caused monetary damage to any individual, partnership, company or corporation, will reimburse that individual when ordered by the real estate commission.

This includes any sales associate or broker who has a valid and active license, who acted as a real estate agent in the transaction, and was not associated with any individual, party, partnership, company or corporation involved in the transaction, so long as the actions of the agent were a violation of this law.

The Real Estate Recovery Fund can also be used, when ordered by the real estate commission, as reimbursement to a sales associate or broker who is required by a court of law to pay damages.

Under no circumstances will funds be given if a sales associate or broker fails to notify the real estate commission in a timely manner.

The Real Estate Recovery Fund is funded in part with a fee of $3.50 for brokers and $1.50 for sales associates, at the time they are issued their first license in addition to the license fee, and at the renewal period of each license annually.

**Section 475.483** pertains to the eligibility and conditions of recovery of funds through the Real Estate Recovery Fund. In the event that a sales associate or broker is legally found to have caused harm during a real estate transaction, any individual is allowed to seek recovery of funds.

- In the event that a sales associate or broker dies and therefore a legal ruling cannot be made, the Florida Real Estate Commission is allowed to waive that requirement.
- If a sales associate or broker files for bankruptcy, he/she is not relieved from having an individual or entity obtain a final judgment against him/her. If this happens, the individual or entity seeking judgment must make the request that the sales associate or broker in question have the assets from the real estate transaction taken out of the bankruptcy proceedings, so that they can be heard in the Florida state court that has jurisdiction over that matter. In the event that a final judgment cannot be reached and the individual or entity loses the asset through the sales associate or broker's bankruptcy, the real estate commission again has the right to waive the requirement of final judgment placed on the individual or entity.

At the time of the occurrence, the individual or entity must notify the real estate commission through certified mail. If no notice is given to the real estate commission, if the commission feels the claim is valid, it can still be honored.

A recovery claim must be made (1) two years or less from the time of the indiscretion that led to the claim, or (2) within two years of the indiscretion being found. In either case, due diligence must be exercised. No claim, under any circumstances, will be honored after more than four years from the occurrence of the indiscretion.

If the sales associate or broker cannot satisfy the judgment in an applicable court of law, then:

- Recovery from persons and alternate sources will be applied to the damages awarded
- Persons aren't precluded from making claims for recovery
- An affidavit showing final judgment isn't appealed/subject of appeal/appeal concluded and outcome rendered

The Real Estate Recovery Fund does not owe an individual or entity recovery if the person in question is the spouse or representative of the sales associate or broker, or is a sales associate or broker who performed duties as a single agent in the damaged transaction claim:

- If the sales associate or broker is the owner or person taking charge of the property in question.
- The sales associate or broker involved did not have a current, active and valid real estate license.

If the claim is described in Section 475.485, Subsection 2, then the real estate commission will pay the attorney fees and court costs of the sales associate or broker that are deemed reasonable, and in the event that the individual or entity wins his/her case, the real estate commission will also cover the attorney fees and court costs deemed reasonable.

**Section 475.4835** refers to the real estate commission's powers upon notification of commencement of action. This means that when the Florida Real Estate Commission gets certified notice of actions, it may intervene by:

- Entering an appearance.
- Filing an answer.
- Defending an action.

The Florida Real Estate Commission may also intervene, on behalf of the State of Florida, to review and rule on the matter.

**Section 475.484** pertains to payments from the Real Estate Recovery Fund. Any individual who meets all of the conditions of Section 475.482 is permitted to apply to the Florida Real Estate Commission for payments to be made from the Real Estate Recovery Fund.

Under Section 475.482, Subsection 1, in the amount equal to, but no more than $50,000 of an unsatisfied judgment, and as it pertains to the Real Estate Recovery Fund, the amount will be equal to the judgment rendered or $50,000, whichever is the lesser value in each case. Recovery will only apply to the actual damages or compensatory damages. Reflecting Section 475.483 "treble damages," any attorney or court fees, as well as any interest on those fees will not be the responsibility of the Real Estate Recovery Fund and will not be covered.

When a claim is received, rights, titles, interest in judgment regarding the payment and all additional payments and fees recovered by the real estate commission's judgment will be used to reimburse the Florida Real Estate Recovery Fund.

Limits will be placed on all claims that come from the same transaction. No matter the number of properties or people involved, the Real Estate Recovery Fund will pay out no more than $50,000 on any one transaction.

Any sales associate or broker is limited to the payouts that the Florida Real Estate Recovery Fund will make over the life of his/her career to the amount of no more than $150,000.

If there is ever a time when the funds in the Real Estate Recovery Fund are too low to cover a valid claim, the real estate commission will cover the unpaid portion as soon as the money can be made available. Additionally, claims will be paid in the order in which they are made.

In the event that, in the course of a real estate commission meeting, a claim is approved that exceeds the lifetime allotment of any one sales associate or broker, the amount approved will be prorated.

The chief financial officer will make all of the payments and disbursements for the Florida Real Estate Recovery Fund, after receipt of a signed voucher from the Department of Business and Professional Regulations' secretary.

As described in Section 475.482, the sales associate or broker against which a claim is made will have his/her license suspended automatically on the date that the payment is made. The license of that sales associate or broker will not be reinstated until the payment for that claim has been repaid in full, plus interest.

There will be no other administrative actions necessary after that point. In the event that a sales associate or broker who has had his/her license suspended owes the Real Estate Recovery Fund for paid claims against him/her, a discharge of bankruptcy will *not* relieve that individual from the penalties or fees owed for this proceeding *except* in the conflict of 11 U.S.C. Section 525 which when it applies, the real estate commission may not discriminate against or suspend the license.

**Section 475.485** pertains to the investment of the Real Estate Recovery Fund. The funds within the recovery fund will be allowed to be invested by the chief financial officer, under the same limitations that apply to investment of other state funds. The interest that is earned off the investment of those funds will be deposited into the Real Estate Recovery Fund, and will be made available for the same purposes and uses as all other money deposited into the fund.

**Section 475.486** rules and violations pertaining to the Florida Real Estate Commission and Florida Department of Business and Professional Regulations. Per subsection 475.482 through 475.486, the real estate commission is permitted to adopt any rules that are necessary to ensure the efficiency of the administration.

Provisions under subsection 475.482 through 475.486 state that it is illegal for any person or agent to file any statements or notices with the Florida Real Estate Commission that are false, contain false materials or make false statements.

Anyone violating this subsection is guilty of a second-degree misdemeanor, punishable under section 775.082 or 775.083.

**Section 475.5015** refers to records in the brokerage business. Per this section, each broker is required to keep and make available to the Department of Business and Professional Regulations any books, accounts and records that will enable the department to decide if a broker is in compliance with the provisions in this section.

Each broker will ensure that a minimum of one legible copy of those books, accounts and records is preserved. Those records must be a full accounting for a minimum of five years from the date any money, funds, deposits, checks, entrusted drafts and/or money received.

If a broker or brokerage's records have been the subject of any litigation, those books, records and accounts are required to be kept for at least two years from the time the civil action concludes and the matter is closed. Under no circumstances will that time exceed the above-mentioned five years.

Under Subsection 475.2755 and 475.278, disclosure documents will be retained by real estate licensees for any and all written contracts for real property purchase and sale transactions.

**Section 475.5016** pertains to the authority to audit and inspect. Agents and employees of the Department of Business and Professional Regulations who are appropriately authorized will have the power to inspect and audit. Those powers will allow them to conduct such business in a lawful manner, during all reasonable hours, within any and all broker or brokerage offices that are licensed under the Florida Real Estate Commission and the Department of Business and Professional Regulations. Such powers will be used to determine provisions and rules under Chapter 455 of Florida Statutes.

**Section 475.5017** pertain to powers related to injunctive relief. This section ensures that the Department of Business and Professional Regulations may have civil action brought in civil court to instruct a broker against their intent, partial involvement or continued involvement whether partial or acting with full intent, of the actions they are committing.

In any event, orders shall be given, or judgment shall be made to ensure the injunction, temporary or permanent, to ensure that the individual doesn't continue his/her misconduct. Additionally, any measures that need to be taken to ensure the enforcement of the injunction will be made available for the enforcement of this injunction.

The jurisdiction and powers of that court will ensure that any of that broker's books, papers, documents and records pertaining to his/her property or business will be retained or restricted to prevent public injury or violation of laws. The individual or individuals receiving any such properties, will be qualified and appointed to take custody, collection, administrative powers, liquidation, etc. of property and business as dictated by the courts. The court may issue orders to stop all pending civil action, court cases and transfer the civil actions to a circuit court judge.

Any expenses will be paid out of the brokerage firm's assets per the approval of the courts. If the assets liquidated are not enough to cover all of the expenses incurred, then the courts may order the Real Estate Recovery Fund to disperse funds up to but not exceeding $100,000 per recipient.

**Section 475.5018** pertains to facsimile signatures or accepted writing. Per this section, a signature or writing, whether physically written or electronically signed, will be binding and legally sufficient.

The above descriptions from Florida statutes chapter 475 .01 through 45.5018 break down the bulk of education, licensing, conduct, misconduct and ramifications for sales associates, brokers and brokerages. This chapter of Florida law also includes the rights and responsibilities of the Florida Real Estate Commission and the Department of Business and Professional Regulations as they pertain to real estate in Florida. More information, including but not limited to commercial real estate, commercial real estate liens and other commercial dealings can be found under Florida statutes Chapter 475.

---

## Florida Fair Housing Law – Florida Statute: Title 44, Chapter 760

The State of Florida established its own state housing law to be run in conjunction with the 1968 Fair Housing Act. Federal law will always supersede

Florida state law if there is ever a conflict between the two. The Florida Americans With Disabilities Accessibility Act was also created to work with the federal ADA to support and enforce federal law.

## Florida Residential Landlord and Tenant Act – Florida Statute: Title 6, Chapter 83

The Residential Landlord and Tenant Act is designed to allow landlords and tenants to have an equitable professional relationship. The law insures residential properties, defined as any property where a person or multiple people live, and prohibits landlords from unfairly imposing rental provisions while simultaneously ensuring their rights as landlords to inspect or enter property without notifying a tenant.

To that end, landlords are required to maintain security deposits and advanced rents in a secure location on the tenants' behalf. The act states:

1. The deposit must be placed in a separate, noninterest bearing, escrow account or
2. In a separate interest-bearing account in which the landlord will owe the tenant interest in the value of either 5% simple interest or 75% of the interest actually earned, as per the landlord's preference
3. The landlord may comingle the deposits with his own funds under the condition that the landlord posts a surety bond with the court clerk in the amount of the deposit or $50,000, whichever is less, and the landlord is required to pay the tenant 5% simple interest.

If the landlord is a licensed real estate agent and acting in that capacity for the property, or a broker is hired by the landlord to act as the property manager, the act will no longer pertain to him/her and will not apply to the deposits covered under the Florida Landlord and Tenant Act. Instead, Florida Real Estate License Law, which can be found under Florida statute 475, will take the act's place.

Landlords are required to maintain the property in normal working order. This includes ensuring that hot water and heat are working properly, and providing pest control.

Tenants are required to keep the property sanitary, maintaining conditions that follow ordinary wear and tear.

When the rental agreement is terminated, the property will be reviewed to determine if any repairs are needed. Landlords are required to notify tenants within 30 days if their security deposit is to be used for repairs or damages. Such notifications must be sent to the tenant by certified mail and the intentional use of the deposit must be outlined in the notice including whether all or part of the deposit is being used, as well as what it's being used for. In the event that the landlord does not follow this process, he/she forfeits the right to any claims on the deposit. In the event that no repairs are needed, landlords are required to return the security deposit within 15 days of the rental agreement being terminated.

If a tenant is in breach of lease, the landlord is fully within his/her rights to evict the tenant. In the event that a landlord breaks the agreement with the tenant, the tenant will be within his/her legal rights to follow the appropriate legal channels in order to get a reduction in rent or to pay rent directly to the court clerk during the litigation process.

## Florida Uniform Land Sales Practice Act – Florida Statute: Title 33, Chapter 498

Under Chapter 5, section 498 of Florida statutes, the Division of Land Sales, Condominiums and Mobile Homes will regulate the sale of all lots in Florida sold for the purposes of building subdivisions and containing 50 lots or more. Public offering statements are required to be provided to prospective buyers within seven days of the purchase contract.

## Florida Do Not Call Law – Florida Statute: Title 33, Chapter 501

While the federal government has a National Do Not Call Registry, the State of Florida also has a similar state law with slightly stricter rules. The Florida law prevents those on the Do Not Call list from being contacted unless the individual or entity is a current or former customer of the company or entity soliciting the call. The exception to the law applies to any For Sale by Owner contacts; those calls can be made without penalty to the solicitor. Aside from this exception, those who violate the law can face fines up to $10,000.

Solicitation calls made to individuals pertaining properties For Sale by Owners do not break Florida law; however, it can be a violation of federal law. Before soliciting a For Sale, real estate agents and brokerage office employees should check both the Florida state registry and the federal registry.

Additionally, effective July 1, 2014, the Florida statute amended the law to include text messaging for sales solicitation.

## Florida Rental List Law – Florida Statute: Title 32, Chapter 475

While this law is outlined above in the breakdown of Chapter 475 of Florida statutes, further explanation is warranted. The Florida Rental List Law pertains to any brokers and sales associates who supply any prospective tenants with a rental information list, at a cost. Specifically, real estate agents must provide current clients with a receipt that indicates their refund rights and under what circumstances those rights apply.

Information on the list must be completely accurate or the prospective tenant or client is entitled to a full refund within 30 days of purchasing the rental list. Additionally, tenants are entitled up to a 75% refund if they do not lease a property through the agent's assistance. That refund is due within 30 days of the list's purchase so long as the prospective tenant or client requests the refund.

Anyone who violates the rental list law can be charged a with first-degree misdemeanor and face fines up to $1,000, up to a year in jail or both.

## Florida Disclosure Law – Florida Statute: Title 32, Chapter 472

Florida state law mandates that all real estate agents disclose specific information pertaining to residential sales to any prospective buyers.

The disclosure laws require that sellers inform prospective and active buyers about matters pertaining to the property that will affect its overall value. These are things that are not openly known or seen by a potential buyer.

Real estate sales associates and brokers must provide written information to prospective and active buyers. The documents are not a guarantee or warranty to the buyer but rather straightforward information. Buyers should still seek professional advice and inspections for any property they are considering purchasing, but this document provides a level of transparency between buyer and seller.

Things that should be disclosed to buyers include but are not limited to:

- Structural issues
- Appliances
- Termites, rodents or other pests
- Organisms or other natural occurrences that may damage the home
- Drainage, flooding or other intrusions of water
- Plumbing, such as drinking water sources
- The lack of a septic system or sewer
- Roofing material
- Systems such as air conditioners, heaters, water heaters
- Amenities such as pools, hot tubs or spas
- Sinkholes or other soil movement or erosion
- Homeowners association restrictions
- Boundaries, or any access roads pertaining to the property
- Environmental notices
- Legislation that may pertain to the property such as zoning
- Legal or administrative claims affecting the property
- Permitted or unpermitted changes to the home such as remodels, improvements or repairs.

Exceptions to this law include new residential homes, apartments and other such residential units. Structures such as these should be in a setting where buyers can see for themselves the state of the property and home. Properties being leased without an option to purchase are not required to provide disclosure documents. Open houses or model homes are also not required to provide disclosure sheets, nor are auctions. An individual performing duties as a transaction broker does not need to provide disclosure sheets either.

Any real estate agent who fails to provide accurate disclosure information to prospective and active buyers may face

- Suspension or revocation of his/her license
- Real estate commission fines

- Legal fines through local and state government
- Disciplinary action
- Legal action in a court of law.

Specific disclosures that must be made if they apply to a given property include:

- Radon gas
- Lead-based paint
- Energy efficiency
- Homeowners association
- Floor insurance
- Condominium or cooperative disclosure.

However, Florida law does not require real estate agents or property owners to disclose information regarding the property pertaining to any stigmas that the property may have acquired. This includes but is not limited to the disclosure of a death, suicide or homicide. Under Florida law these do not have to be disclosed since they do not affect the property's value in a material way.

**Financial Institution Reform, Recovery and Enforcement Act of 1989 – FIRREA – Florida Statute: Title 32, Chapter 475**

This law requires that appraisals for the sale or purchase of federally related transactions be conducted by an appraiser who is properly educated, certified and licensed through the State of Florida. The specific requirements for education can be found in Chapter 475 of the Florida statutes under the part which pertains to the real estate appraisal board, appraiser educational requirements and licensing requirements.

Uniform standard and professional appraisal practices (USPAPs) bar sales associates, broker associates and brokers from performing appraisals unless an individual holds an appraiser's license in addition to a real estate license.

By this standard an appraiser can properly evaluate, support and estimate the overall value of a property. The appraisal will be good as of the date it was done to attest to the home's value. This value may include the:

- Investment value

- Assessed value
- Liquidation value
- Salvage value
- Insurable value, or
- Market value.

## Florida Homestead Act or Florida Homestead Tax Exemption – Florida Statute: Title 14, Chapter 196

Under Florida law, a property owner who is a permanent resident or the permanent resident of a dependent may be eligible to receive the homestead tax exemption. This exemption allows up to $50,000 in tax exemptions towards a permanent primary residence. The first $25,000 applies to all property taxes, including but not limited to taxes for the school district the property is located in. Additional exemptions may be applied up to $25,000 if the value of the property is between $50,000 and $75,000. This exemption applies to personal property taxes excluding those pertaining to the school district the property is in.

In order to qualify for this tax exemption, property owners are required to complete forms through the State of Florida's revenue office. These forms will request information including the title holder's name, social security number, spouse's social security number (if applicable) and information on any dependents living in the owner's home as of January of the year the exemption is claimed for.

## Florida Green Belt Laws – Florida Statute: Title 14, Chapter 193

Florida has a special interest in agricultural property owners that may face financial issues. The Florida Green Belt Law entitles owners of agricultural properties to tax credits, exemptions and breaks. Agricultural properties are assessed for their agricultural purpose, which generally lowers the value and qualifies the owner for tax exemptions. Agricultural property owners must apply for these exemptions on an annual basis.

## Florida Statute of Fraud Law – Florida Statute: Title 39, Chapter 680

The State of Florida requires that binding agreements or contracts be in writing in order to be considered valid. To that end, real estate brokers and sales associates must have written agreements between themselves and their clients. This is done as a means to prevent fraud from either party. These agreements must be drafted when a sale of real property is made, as well as any long-term lease of property. These agreements must clearly state terms of sale, terms of a lease, restrictions and any other important claims. All parties must agree to the full contract before it is signed.

## Florida Foreclosure Law – Florida Statute: Title 40, Chapter 702

Foreclosures in the State of Florida are a judicial process. This requires that lenders file lawsuits in state court against borrowers. Once a complaint is submitted to the courts, the borrower will be served. Borrowers are granted 20 days to file an answer with the state court in response to the lender's complaint. Those who do not respond by that deadline may find a default judgment granted to the lender.

If an excuse for nonpayment or a justification presented with a counterclaim is not given, then the state is almost guaranteed to rule in the lender's favor. In rare cases, a judge may deny a lender's motion which will forward the case on to discovery and trial, which puts a temporary halt to the foreclosure until that process is concluded.

Florida law does allow for foreclosures to be moved more quickly if the borrower does not contest the lender's complaint.

Once Florida state courts rule in favor of the lender for foreclosure, the property will be placed for sale 20 to 35 days from the time the judgment is made. Florida statute 45.031 requires that the sale of the home must be published publicly in a newspaper for two consecutive weeks, and the second publication must be made a minimum of five days prior to the property's sale.

In foreclosure proceedings in the State of Florida, a home will be auctioned and sold to the highest bidder. The county clerk's office must file a certificate of sale under Florida statute 45.031, usually by the next business day.

The previous homeowner must move out before or at the time of sale. In the event that the previous owner doesn't move out by the time the property is sold, the new owner may offer what is called a cash-for-keys deal or begin eviction proceedings against the previous owner.

## Community Planning Act – Florida Statute: Title 40, Chapter 163

This law, enacted in 2011, puts local government in charge of community development, rather than the Department of Community Affairs, which had previously held the responsibility. Today community planning is run by the division of community development.

Law zoning, land use restrictions and building codes are managed under this act. Zoning laws were put in place to define five specific types of zoning which include residential, commercial, industrial, agricultural and special use zones.

For the health and safety of the community, building codes ensure the quality and methods of any construction. Local government requires a certificate of occupancy before a building can be occupied by anyone. This inspection is done before the building is opened and includes ensuring that residential and commercial facilities have:

- Fire-proofing
- Ventilation
- Wind-load strength
- Restrooms
- Other features pertaining to community safety.

A health ordinance is also in place regarding commercial use properties. Restaurants, bars, grocery stores, taverns, public water and sewer, as well as the vast array of other commercial use buildings are required to meet health department regulations locally. while some exceptions do apply.

## Florida Marketable Record Title Act 1963 – Florida Statute: Title 40, Chapter 712

This act was created to place 30-year limits on specific defects to a title. The law states that in the event the continued chain of title was kept on any given property for at least 30 years any defects to that title prior to the 30-year mark are cured and no longer valid. To help with this, titles that are reviewed and deemed markable allow for owners and lenders to purchase title insurance for their protection. There are two forms of title insurance:

- **Owner's policy title insurance**: Commonly called a mortgagor's policy, this is compiled based on a property's purchase price and covers all claims made against the property up to the policy's face value. Owner's policies are nontransferable. If new owners want title insurance, they must purchase it on their own.
- **Lender's policy title insurance**: Also called a mortgagee's policy, this is required by the lender if a property has a mortgage on it. The lender's policy protects the lender's investment and can be transferred to other lenders in the event that a mortgage is bought out, sold or refinanced to a different lender.

## Federal Laws

**Civil Rights Act of 1866-1968**

The United States Civil Rights Act was established in 1866 to abolish discrimination based on race. In 1964 the act was expanded to encompass race, color, religion, sex and national origin. It also was expanded to include voting, employment and public accommodations. In 1968 the law was revised in an effort to strengthen nondiscrimination in real property. The Civil Rights Act of 1968 includes the Fair Housing Act, which expanded the law to forbid housing discrimination based on race, color, religion, sex and national origin.

**The Fair Housing Act 1968**

The Fair Housing Act of 1968 includes single and multifamily homes. More specifically it pertains to residential property that is not privately owned; privately owned residential property that is being sold, purchased, or leased through a real estate agent; property owners who rent residential units of four or more, and those who, in a two-year period, sell two or more homes that they do not live in when the property is sold.

In 1988, the Fair Housing Act was amended to include handicapped individuals and families with children. This law pertains to those who are either physically or mentally impaired to the point that it hinders typical day-to-day activities. The law was expanded to include minor children and pregnant women.

Exceptions to the Fair Housing Act include retirement communities for residents 62 years of age or older, and any development which has at least 80% of its units or homes occupied by those who are 55 years of age or older. Search developments are required to provide senior citizens with activities that are appropriate for their age and stage of life.

Generally speaking, the Fair Housing Act does not apply to any individual or couple selling a home they currently live in through a For Sale by Owner in which they represent themselves. So long as the homeowner is representing him/herself and is selling an individual home, the Fair Housing Act does not apply. However, the Civil Rights Act of 1866 does apply and prevents discrimination against race.

Under the Fair Housing Act, property owners and brokers are not allowed to:

- Refuse a sale, lease or negotiations to those protected under the Fair Housing Act.
- Quote terms, conditions or prices differently based on the terms outlined in the Fair Housing Act.
- Utilize steering, which involves discouraging or encouraging an individual protected by the Fair Housing Act to/from properties.
- Blockbusting, which refers to selling or renting properties in specific areas due to demographics.
- Barring those protected under the FHA from accessing MLS numbers or other marketing systems for discriminatory reasons.
- Making inaccurate statements regarding a property's availability of sale or lease due to discriminatory reasons.
- Acting in a manner commonly known as "redlining," which refers to withholding real estate services or mortgages to people protected under the FHA because of the geographic location in which they reside.

The Fair Housing Act is upheld by HUD. An individual or group of individuals must file a complaint with HUD in regard to any discrimination that occurs. It will be up to that individual or group of individuals to prove discrimination. If violence is involved, the charges are then taken to federal court.

Real estate agents need to be vigilant that any conversations they engage in, requests to see specific homes and/or showing of specific properties is not based upon race, color, religion, sex, national origin, family status, sexual orientation or a handicap.

## Americans with Disabilities act 1990

In 1990, the Americans with Disabilities Act (ADA) was put into place. This law requires that handicapped individuals have access to public transportation, commercial facilities and other community and public accommodations. New construction, as well as renovations, is required to meet specific ADA codes.

## The Interstate Land Sales Full Disclosure Act

This act pertains to the sale of property that is made up of 25 lots or more. Such sales require that a property report be provided to any prospective buyers a minimum of three days before a purchase agreement is made. A seven-day window to rescind an offer is given to every prospective buyer in the event that a property report is not provided in a timely manner. Buyers are given 24 months to rescind a contract, with a full refund of any deposit.

## Comprehensive Environmental Response, Compensation and Liability Act – CERCLA

This act, enacted in 1980, pertains to hazardous substances in properties that pose a risk to public safety. State agencies also have additional laws and regulations pertaining to environmental hazards and responsibility. The national priorities list (NPL) was created in order to identify contaminated sites properties so they can be cleaned up.

## Superfund Amendment and Reauthorization Act – SARA

In 1986, CERCLA was amended to become SARA. Funds are now gained through a variety of taxes placed upon chemical products and petroleum products.

The government wants to ensure that anyone responsible for hazardous substances is held accountable. To that end, the government has made this law broad, to cover a wide range for those who could be liable for cleanup of any contaminated site.

Responsible parties include but are not limited to:

- The owner of the site that is contaminated
- Former owners, if the site was contaminated during the time they owned the property
- Manufacturers of hazardous substances, or
- Those who transport hazardous substances.

## Federal Income Tax Laws

The federal government allows the IRS to collect taxes for properties sold which received capital gains. When the federal government collects taxes, it also offers tax breaks to homeowners. This includes capital gains from a primary residence when it is sold. Additional advantages to home ownership include a mortgage interest deduction, property tax deduction or IRS withdrawal.

Principle residency sales can qualify for a taxpayer's foreign exclusion of up to $250,000 for single individuals or those who are married and filing separate, and up to $500,000 for married couples filing jointly. The mortgage interest deduction allows the taxpayer to deduct from the first or second home mortgage the interest paid for that year. The property tax deduction allows homeowners to deduct the property taxes paid on a first or second home for the year. First-time homebuyers may make a tax-free withdrawal from an IRA account when it is used towards the down payment of their first home on an amount not to exceed $10,000.

## National Do Not Call Registry List

Cold-calling is something sales associates, brokers and other brokerage employees need to be careful of. The Federal Communications Commission (FCC) established the National Do Not Call Registry in 2003. The list allows the public to sign up if they do not wish telemarketers to contact them. The FCC manages the list and is also responsible for enforcing the laws for anyone who violates it. Violations can result in up to $11,000 in fines.

Organizations calling for political reasons, charity organizations, telephone surveys and companies who have already established business relationships with individuals or entities are exempt from penalty. Additionally, if an individual or entity has submitted an application to a company or entity, or made a business transaction, these calls are also exempt. Individuals who submit applications can be contacted as long as it is within 90 days of the application being submitted, and those who have conducted business with a company or entity are allowed to be contacted up to 18 months after their business transaction.

## Home Mortgage Disclosure Act

This act requires financial agencies to maintain, report and publicly share loan information regarding mortgages. This data assists in showing whether lenders are meeting the needs of the communities they are operating within. This helps public officials and governing bodies with decision- and policy-making. It also allows regulators to take note of any potential discrimination. All information disclosed under the Home Mortgage Disclosure Act is altered to protect a borrower's personal information.

## Capital Gains Exclusion or Home Sales Tax Exclusion

This act allows homeowners who sell their main home to get a tax break on money earned from the sale. Money earned refers to any funds earned after the balance of any existing mortgage on the home has been paid off and brought to a zero balance.

The IRS allows homeowners who meet IRS requirements to have a portion of the earnings from their home excluded from taxes. For married couples, the full amount that can be excluded is $500,000. For unmarried individuals, the full amount that can be excluded is $250,000.

To qualify for the Home Sales Tax Exclusion:

1. The home that is sold *must* be a person's primary residence for a minimum of two years over a five-year period, and
2. The person must not have been given a Home Sales Tax Exclusion in the past 24 months.

Some people who don't meet those two requirements will still qualify for a tax exemption on at least a portion of the money earned from the sale. Those who own multiple homes will have more to consider.

The IRS instructs those seeking the Home Sales Tax Exclusion that the house that they use the majority of the time is the one that will be considered their "main" home. If you have a home that you:

- Use as your mailing address

- Use on important documents such as tax returns
- Us located near family and/or friends you see often, or
- Is located close to your work or primary office,

then consideration may be applied to that property.

## Mortgage Interest Deductions

This is a tax deduction that applies to mortgage interest paid on the debt for up until the first $1,000,000 of a mortgage. Main homes can be properties such as a house, condo, apartment, mobile home, trailer home or houseboat. In order to qualify as a home, a property must contain

- Sleeping quarters
- Cooking facilities
- Toileting facilities.

A home mortgage that is obtained to "buy out" a spouse or significant other in divorce proceedings can also be eligible for the tax cut.

Those who qualify for a military or ministry housing allowance that is nontaxable can still qualify for a home mortgage deduction.

Those who have purchased a home after December 15, 2017, will be allowed to use up to the first $750,000 in interest on any given mortgage as well. It's important to know that in order to utilize this deduction, a person must itemize his/her tax return.

Keeping accurate and detailed records is always important when seeking any deductions.

Deductions that cannot be used include

- Homeowners insurance
- Payments made on the principle in addition to the standard mortgage payment agreement
- Title insurance
- Forfeited money for earnest money/deposits/down payments
- Reverse mortgage interest.

## Federal Foreclosure Laws

The United States federal government has several laws pertaining to foreclosures. Under U.S. Title 12, banks and banking you will find Chapter 38 A, single family mortgage foreclosures; in Chapter 38 you will also find multifamily mortgage foreclosures.

In addition to these foreclosure laws there are federal laws that went into place on January 10, 2014, to protect homeowners during the foreclosure process. These laws ensure that assistance can be offered to borrowers in the event that they are having a hard time making their mortgage payments. The laws also protect borrowers from wrongful actions by lenders.

Federal government laws help borrowers retain their property by working out alternate mortgage payment arrangements. The laws offer lenders the same procedures on a federal level to execute foreclosures as necessary.

## Equal Credit Opportunity Act – ECOA

This act was established in 1974 and forbids public assistance programs from prohibiting financial assistance to individuals based on race, religion, age, sex, marital status, sexual orientation or national origin.

## Consumer Credit Protection Act – TILA

The Truth in Lending Act provides all borrowers with disclosures regarding the cost associated with borrowing. This includes interest rates and other charges associated with borrowing. The annual percentage rate (APR) must be clearly disclosed by lenders to borrowers no more than three business days after receiving their application. This law pertains to all consumer loans, not just those regarding real estate.

## Real Estate Settlement Procedures Act – RESPA

All loans that are related to the federal government are protected by this act. This provides all borrowers with full disclosure regarding closing costs for buying a home. Lenders must provide applicants with an informational booklet and a good faith estimate of closing costs. The act also prohibits lenders from being compensated through referral fees or kickbacks from closing costs unless actual services are provided.

## TILA /RESPA Integrated Disclosure or Closing Disclosure Law

This law, enacted by the Consumer Financial Protection Bureau, requires lenders to provide borrowers with a TILA/RESPA closing disclosure at least three days before closing.

## Fraud Enforcement and Recovery Act – FERA

In 2009 the federal government expanded federal law enforcement officials' power to enforce laws against mortgage fraud. This law can include fines up to $1,000,000 and 30 years in prison. States also have the right to their own laws regarding mortgage fraud that can be applied in addition to federal law. There are two main categories which federal law enforcement looks at regarding fraud in mortgages.

1. Fraud for housing refers to borrowers who submit information that is untrue or incomplete so that they may qualify for a loan or be given better terms when purchasing a home.
2. Fraud for profit refers to real estate professionals such as appraisers or brokers who commit fraud as a means to gain money on the purchase or sale of a property, those funds being secured by falsifying information to increase a property's value, commission earned or other ways of securing additional funds that are not justified.

Some of the most common tactics used for mortgage fraud include fraudulent support documents, property flipping, straw buyers, silent second, stolen identity and inflated appraisals.

More than one third of states in the US have laws pertaining to mortgage fraud, including Florida. Federal sentences tend to be much harsher than those issued at the state level.

# Chapter 7: Information for Sales Associates

As a real estate sales associate, you will be entering the field at the bottom. Real estate is a complex business and there are a lot of things you need to know before you are ready to undertake such a position.

A good place to start is to understand real estate as a business. In this business a sales associate is given a safety net. How so? Because all sales associates are supervised and operate under the supervision of a broker. The broker you work under is liable for your actions, so both you and your broker will work together to help you learn the field of real estate.

The Florida Real Estate Commission and the Florida Department of Business and Professional Regulations will be two organizations that you need to make yourself very familiar with. These two organizations oversee and set the guidelines for realtors, as well as handle complaints, violations and disciplinary actions. Your pre-licensing education requirements, licensing exams, post-licensing education, license renewals and much more are all handled through these entities.

All real estate agents need to have a vast knowledge of the real estate world and how it works. Property transfers, marketing conditions, marketing and sales will all be important components in your career ahead.

When it comes to real estate, sales and leasing of property in the State of Florida make up a large part of the business you will be conducting on a regular basis. As a sales associate you will either work for an individual broker or you will work under a brokerage that has one or more brokers. In many cases you will work alongside one or more sales associates who also work under that broker or brokerage.

While working under a broker or brokerage you will work out of either a branch or broker's office. By federal law, brokers are required to register their office. Part of that requirement is the sign that is required to be either on the front door of the office or located close to the front entrance. This sign will clearly state the name of a brokerage if it has one, the name of the broker as it appears on the real estate license and "licensed real estate broker" must be clearly legible on the sign as well. Sales associates are not required to have their names listed on such signage. Some brokers and brokerages choose to list their sales associates and the license they hold on the sign as well.

While sales associates are not permitted to work directly with individuals, entities or the community, you will learn how to run a lot of the business' day-to-day operations and as you prove yourself, you will be delegated more responsibilities by your supervisors. Ultimately, your broker will supervise your work and be legally responsible for your actions. With that in mind, you should be sure to ask questions to ensure that the information you provide to the public and the work that you execute is done to the best of your ability, and also to the legal standard required by your position.

Escrow accounts are something that you will become familiar with as a sales associate. While sales associates are not legally allowed to maintain escrow accounts, the broker or brokerage which they work for may be responsible for maintaining them. Sales associates make deposits in their broker or brokerage's name. If, for any reason, a check is made out to a sales associate, the sales associate should endorse the check, and immediately submit it to the broker. This can include deposits, earnest money, security deposits, first and last month's rent or other fees associated with the rental of a property. All of these funds should always be given to a broker immediately for deposit.

Some sales associates, brokers or brokerages will focus their energy on a specific area within their community. This style of specialization is known as a "farm area" and allows the real estate agent to learn that specific area well in order to give the most up-to-date information on that area when showing properties to prospective buyer or renters.

In real estate there are five specific sales areas:

1. Residential
2. Commercial
3. Industrial
4. Agricultural, and
5. Business real.

In addition to your role in sales and purchasing of real estate you may also find yourself in the business of property management. As a property manager you may be handling properties that an individual or entity is selling or buying, or you may be managing residential or commercial properties that are for rent.

In those categories you are sure to come into contact with condominium properties, time-share properties, cooperatives, homeowners associations (HOAs) and property owners associations (POA). All of these come with additional fees, generally on an annual basis, that potential buyers will need information on. Disclosing specific information to potential buyers will help them to make an educated decision on a purchase. The fees generally provide the owners with amenities, cost-sharing or other advantages that make them desirable to ensure that homeowners will be open to purchasing properties that have such conditions attached to them.

While sales associates and brokers cannot appraise properties in Florida unless individuals have an appraiser's license, sales associates and brokers often conduct a "comparative market analysis" to help property owners evaluate their area, compare the sale of similar properties and assist in finding a fair market price to list homes for sale, lease or rent.

Sales associates also need to be familiar with real estate financing. While you won't do the actual financing yourself or through your brokerage, you will need to be able to assist your clients in knowing where to look and how to go about applying for financing. This is especially true for anyone who is a first-time buyer.

Acquiring land, development purchases, subdivision purchases, new construction purchases and remodels will be things that you see throughout your career. You should be familiar with three styles of residential construction:

- Speculative
- Tract,
- Custom.

The State of Florida, through the Division of Real Estate, only offers real estate licenses for sales associates and brokers. A broker associate is an individual with a license as a broker, but who continues to work under a broker's supervision.

Licensed sales associates are required to complete post-licensing education during the first year of licensing, and continued education for all renewals of future licensing. Sales associates are required to complete a 45-hour post-licensing course and successfully pass the exam at the end of the course. This post-licensing education *must* be completed *before* a license is up for renewal. After that first year, sales associates are required to complete 14 hours of continued education each year before their license is due for renewal. This continued education keeps sales associates up-to-date on city codes, state and federal laws and other changes that apply to real estate sales and property management.

For those who do not live in Florida but wish to work as real estate associates there, Florida is part of a "mutual recognition" with Alabama, Georgia, Indiana, Mississippi, Nebraska, Tennessee, Arkansas, Oklahoma and Connecticut. This provision allows those educated and licensed in those states to qualify for the same license in Florida by passing a 40-question exam with a 75% or higher.

Regardless of the license you seek, Florida's Department of Business and Professional Regulations handles the regulation of most professional licenses, including those for real estate sales associates and brokers, under Florida statute Chapter 455. The Department of Business and Professional Regulations contains the:

- Division of Technology, Licensure and Testing
- Division of Regulations, with authority to investigate and execute legal matters
- Division of Professions, pertaining to state boards and commissions; and
- Division of Real Estate, which supports the Florida Real Estate Commission.

A real estate license can be labeled as effective, ineffective, canceled, suspended, involuntary inactive, cease to be in force, void, revoked or expired.

1. **Effective:** All forms are submitted properly so that the license is current and valid. This can also pertain to active or voluntary inactive licenses.
2. **Ineffective:** The individual has a license but is barred from using it.
3. **Canceled:** A broker resigns, dies or does not renew a license. If this occurs, any sales associates working under that broker will also have their license made involuntarily inactive until they are hired to work under a new broker.

4. **Suspended:** The license is suspended for 10 years or less, due to penalties against the license holder. During this time the individual is barred from practicing in the real estate field.
5. **Involuntarily inactive:** When a broker loses his/her license through a suspension or having had it revoked, sales associates working under that broker's supervision will temporarily be unable to use their license until they are properly hired under a new broker.
6. **Cease to be in Force:** When a broker or brokerage has a change of address, they are given 10 days to inform the Division of Real Estate. Failure to do so will cause a license, as well as any licenses under their supervision to be unusable until the situation can be rectified.
7. **Void:** Any time a license is revoked or expires it becomes void.
8. **Revoked:** The license is lost temporarily, per the Florida Real Estate Commission's orders.
9. **Revoked:** The Florida Real Estate Commission permanently takes an individual's license.
10. **Expired:** Any time the proper forms are not submitted, and a license is not properly renewed by or before its expiration date it becomes expired and is invalid for use.

As a real estate agent, it is important for you to understand your product. Real estate is defined as land (actual surface area) and all permanent structures, improvements and environment (trees, rock formations, etc.) Within that scope there are a slew of things real estate encompasses. These included but are not limited to land (the actual physical area of any property), real property (all physical elements including air rights, surface rights and subsurface rights), water rights and water restrictions.

Surface rights pertain to the physical land and anything that is attached to it permanently such as structures, fence lines and waterways.

Subsurface rights pertain to things that are under the physical surface area of the property such as oil and minerals.

Air rights pertain to the area that is directly above any given property.

In the State of Florida, real property refers to physical land, structures and assets (both tangible and intangible). However, personal property refers to any property that is tangible, movable and often has a shelf life. The most basic principle of ownership regarding any given property is that an individual or entity owns the physical land as well as structures on it, and there are some rights that inherently belong to the property owner. 'Chattel' is often another word that is used in reference to personal property.

Real estate agents sometimes deal with properties where the owner has died. For properties like this, sales associates will need to be familiar with wills and deeds.

A will is a set of written instructions, in some cases transfers of property, after the individual has died. It can also furnish other details regarding real and personal properties.

A deed is proof of ownership, in writing, that is a legal binding decree of ownership. This is needed when transferring property after a death.

Florida state law makes concessions for properties whose owners do not have a will and have no living family. In cases like this the ownership of the property defaults to the State of Florida. For any deeds to be legally valid, certain requirements must be met. These requirements include:

- The deed must be in writing
- It must contain the name of any and all grantors or grantees
- It must contain the granting clause defining the estate type through a habendum clause
- It must be signed by a competent grantor in front of two or more subscribed witnesses, and
- The deed must be delivered and accepted by the grantee.

In real estate there are many forms of deeds. These deeds may include but are not limited to:

- Statutory deeds
- Quitclaim deeds
- Bargain and sale deeds
- Special warranty deeds
- General warranty deeds
- Guardian deeds, and

- Committee deeds.

While deeds show proof of ownership, the United States federal government, Florida state government and local government have laws, restrictions and codes that to an extent dictate what an owner is or is not allowed to do with property. Specifically, those limitations fall into three categories.

1. The first category pertains to police powers which allow government to set laws and restrictions for the general welfare, safety and health of its communities and those that live there.
2. The second category is eminent domain. Eminent domain grants the government permission to take property from owners when it is going to be used for public purposes. Under eminent domain, the government must financially compensate all property owners at a fair value that is determined through a court of law.
3. The third category is taxation. This allows the government to require property owners to pay taxes on the property which they own. The government may also issue penalties when those taxes are not paid, allow liens to be placed on properties and in worst-case scenarios force property owners into a public sale of their property if those taxes are not paid.

As a sales associate, knowing how a buyer's market or seller's market operates, the supply and demand in your area and the vacancy rate pertaining to the purchase, sale and rental of property will be very important.

When the market is flooded with real estate but buying is down, you're in a buyer's market. This allows potential homebuyers to have more room to negotiate their purchase price. On the other hand, when there is very little inventory, and a high number of buyers, then you are in a seller's market. If you're selling a property in a buyer's market, this can be a great advantage. With very few properties and multiple buyers, the purchase price of a property can be driven well above the asking price.

Conducting a comparative market analysis can help you to inform clients who are selling property regarding the best fair market value. You must ensure that a list price is high enough that the property owner won't take a loss, but also low enough that prospective buyers will see it as fair and have interest in the property.

When buying and selling real estate, it's also important to know tax rates, tax laws, tax exemptions and additional tax deductions. In some cases, both buyers and sellers have access to unique tax breaks when buying a first home, selling a primary home or using property for agricultural purposes. For more on those laws, see the section above regarding state and federal laws.

In real estate one of the most common documents you will come in contact with are contracts. You will prepare purchase contracts, sales contracts, listing agreements, property management contracts, rental agreement or leases, as well as other office-related contracts that pertain to your brokerage.

As a real estate agent, you will need to be familiar with the following types of contracts:

- Bilateral
- Unilateral
- Expressed contracts
- Implied contracts
- Executed contracts
- Executory contracts
- Formal contracts, and
- Informal contracts.

Contracts pertaining to the purchase or sale of real estate should include:

- Date
- Time
- Closing location
- Price at which the property is purchased
- Any legal descriptions pertaining to the property
- Terms of the financing for the property
- State and quality of the title that is being conveyed
- Type of deed that's involved with the purchase
- Any personal property that is being included in the purchase
- Any necessary title evidence
- Closing costs
- Taxes
- Any dues for HOAs

- POs or condominium fees
- Rent, if it applies
- Any other fees or deposits.

When purchasing real estate, it's important to familiarize yourself with available financing. While you will not be directly involved with the financing, you need to be informed on what's available to potential buyers in order to be able to advise them.

Mortgages available include:

- Amortized
- Adjustable rate
- Partially amortized
- Biweekly
- Package
- Blanket
- Purchase money
- Reverse annuity
- Term, and
- Conventional mortgages.

There are also home equity loans, land contract loans, federal housing administration loans (FHA loans) and VA loans for veterans who qualify.

Loans can be secured in a variety of ways including savings and loan associations, commercial banks, credit unions, mortgage bankers and mortgage brokers. Private funding and government programs are also resources to consider when financing a home. When local lenders do not have enough funding to cover your purchase or you're seeking alternative options, there's also a secondary mortgage market. These lenders include the Federal National Mortgage Association (FNMA), the Government National Mortgage Association (GNMA) and the Federal Home Loan Mortgage Corporation (FHLMC). You should be familiar with all of these.

Whether you're selling a property for someone or showing properties to prospective buyers, city planning and zoning will be an important factor depending on the properties involved. Planning and zoning distinguishes residential and commercial areas, rural and residential areas, agricultural and industrial areas and special zoning. Volume selling in the Sunshine State provides prospective real estate owners with the unique oceanfront properties and everglade properties that Florida has to offer. Zoning will play an important part in this since many properties have special conditions regarding property ownership along the waterfront as well as environmental protections.

Learning all of this information in detail is an extraordinary task. As a sales associate you have much to learn before you acquire your license. This book will help you to grasp the concepts, terms, laws, codes and information you will need in your efforts to become a real estate sales associate.

# Chapter 8: Information for Brokers

As a broker, you are choosing to take on a great deal more responsibility, and even greater liability than you did as a sales associate. As a broker you will not only be responsible for yourself but also for the sales associates who work under your supervision. Your job will entail helping them to fully grasp the world of real estate and all that it entails. You will also be held liable for their smallest infractions as well any more serious mistakes.

There are many things you need to know in order to become a licensed broker in the State of Florida. This includes understanding how to start, own and operate a real estate office. You will be responsible for managing escrow accounts, handling the valuation of real estate, organizing property appraisals, conducting comparative market analyses and valuing businesses. You will have to understand the fine points of contracts, have a full understanding of real estate financing, real estate closing, real estate tax laws and real estate investments, as well as planning, zoning and environmental issues. You will also need to be well versed in property management. Some of this information you will already be familiar with from working as a sales associate.

In order to become a real estate broker in the State of Florida you are first required to complete 72 hours of pre-licensing education courses. The Florida Real Estate Commission has a course for individuals wishing to become brokers. Assuming that you become a licensed real estate broker there are post-licensing education requirements and continue education requirements. Post-licensing education courses must be done before your license expires the first year you are licensed. This gives you 12 months from the time you receive your license. After your first broker's license renewal you will be required to complete 14 hours of continued education each year to ensure that you are up-to- date on the most current information, codes and laws that pertain to the real estate field.

As a broker you are required to maintain a principal office that you work out of. This can be an office in your home or a commercial property that you have purchased or rented for the use of your main office. There are several ways that this can be done, including a sole proprietorship, general partnership, limited partnership, limited liability partnership, corporation or a limited liability company.

As you decide how to start your real estate office as a broker or to develop a brokerage, creating a business plan may be your first step. Consider start-up costs and the capital you may need. Finding a location, managing the cost associated with that and setting up an office and the cost of doing so are also important things to consider. Ensuring that your office is properly equipped will be incredibly important to your business. This includes the systems you use for your phone and internet services, equipment such as computers and copy machines, and office furniture. How well you equip your business will reflect on your company and will in part determine how well you succeed.

Deciding whether you want to be an independent company, work for an already established brokerage or join a franchise are important things to consider when starting off as a real estate broker. Remember that you're in charge, so you will be responsible for hiring any necessary management staff, HR staff or support staff. Remember, before hiring staff you will need to know what services you require and must establish an application and vetting process.

Designing your application process and deciding how you will choose candidates that are right for you is very important. Require applicants to tell you about qualifications that they feel are necessary for success in the business and see if they fit your needs and vision. During a second interview, be prepared to go over your brokerage policies and further discuss the details of what would be required should the individual be hired. A second interview may be the time to introduce prospective employees to current employees that work for you such as support staff, management staff, sales associates or brokers if you have hired any of those staff members yet.

When you're ready to hire, ensure that you have an employment contract. Generally, these employment agreements include provisions for the individual to be an independent contractor. Also include noncompete clauses, protection for client lists, trade secrets and other skills preventing those you hire from taking skills they learn within your company to someone else's business. Also outline terms for commissions.

It's important to create a standardized training process for all employees so there is no confusion as to how things should run and the procedures that should be followed. Compose a manual for policies and procedures that includes the policies and procedures for your business, codes pertaining to the Florida Real Estate Commission in the Department of Business and Professional Regulations, as well as provisions pertaining to local, state and federal laws. Your policy manual should include:

- A mission statement, philosophy and goals
- Provisions for how commissions are calculated and distributed
- Office policies
- Job responsibilities
- Responsibilities regarding open houses
- Procedures on how phone calls and emails should be answered and responded to
- Outlines for how sales meetings should be conducted
- Responsibilities for advertising
- Expenses within the business
- Personal safety expectations
- Confidentiality requirements, and
- Provisions for the Equal Opportunity Employment laws.

As a broker, your office, as well as any branch offices, must have an official brokerage sign that meets Florida Real Estate Commission standards. If your brokerage company has the name that should be listed on the sign, your name as it appears on your license must be listed, and the sign must read "licensed real estate broker." The sign is required to either be on your front door or very close to your front door and in plain view. Additionally, you may choose to add real estate sales associates or broker associates who worked under your supervision to your sign. If you decide to add sales associates or broker associates, their names as they appear on their licenses and the license title that they hold are adequate representation.

As a real estate broker, advertising for your services falls under the jurisdictional umbrella of the Florida Real Estate Commission. Your responsibility is to ensure that any advertising you do is done in a way that does not mislead, omit, deceive or outright lie to the general public in any way.

As a broker it is your job to ensure that local, state and federal laws are upheld within your office, while conducting business and by those who work under your supervision. Ensure that you follow fair housing and advertising laws which fall under HUD and the Fair Housing Act. You will also need to know state and federal Do-Not Call Registry protocols and how to check those lists when conducting business. You will also be bound by federal laws that apply to calls made regarding For Sale by Owner properties.

As a real estate broker, part of your job will be holding deposits and valued items belonging to others in your trust. Though brokers are not bound by law to have an escrow account, the majority use commercial banks, savings banks or credit unions in order to hold escrow funds and conduct their business. Doing so is the most reliable way to account for the funds that you are managing for others.

All funds that a broker is responsible for are required to be deposited within three business days from the time they are received. Under Florida laws this is referred to as immediate deposit. The sales associates or broker associates that work under your supervision are required to turn over any funds received no more than 24 hours after receiving them. Sales associates and broker associates are also allowed to deposit funds directly into the escrow account so long as the broker is informed and approves of them doing so.

Brokers are required to keep detailed, accurate records. Some of these records include monthly cash receipts and cash disbursements, a master journal, a statement of monthly reconciliations, individual customer ledger sheets and the master customer ledger. It's important that these records are kept up to date and in great detail. The Department of Business and Professional Regulations has the power to inspect such records at any reasonable time that falls within regular business hours.

Monthly statements of reconciliation should include the following bare minimum information:

- Reconciliation date
- Date on which the balance was reconciled
- Name of the bank
- Name on the account
- Account number
- Account balance and date on which the balance was obtained
- List of any outstanding checks

- Itemized list of trust liabilities
- Deposits in transit, and
- Relevant miscellaneous data that pertains to the reconciliation.

In addition to keeping records, brokers need to ensure that their offices follow state and federal guidelines. Brokerage offices can be routinely inspected to ensure that those laws and codes are being properly adhered to. During a routine inspection there is a set of minimum office requirements that every inspector will be looking for. Those requirements include:

- The broker's office entrance sign, as described above
- Licenses and registration for the brokerage, any brokers in the firm and any sales associates within the firm
- Any other relevant employee information
- Agency disclosure, which means that the broker must be able to produce agency policies upon request by the inspector.

Brokers need to keep accurate and up-to-date information on all escrow accounts. The Department of Business and Professional Regulations will conduct audits on those escrow accounts. There's no specific time frame on if/when audits will be done and no notice will be given, so it's important that escrow accounts and their records be maintained at all times. Documents that you will need to provide during the auditing process include:

- List of liabilities
- Bank statements for the past six months
- Lease and rental agreements for any rental audits
- Canceled checks collected over the past six months
- Reconciliation records for the past six months
- Signed monthly broker statements
- Checkbook and deposit receipts
- A report on all current banking activities
- The agreement for interest-bearing escrow accounts.

Once the audit commences, the investigator will complete a review of the following information:

- Bank statements, looking for any bank charges, insufficient funds and negative balances
- Reconciliation bank statements
- Canceled checks
- Deposit slips
- Monthly reconciliations
- Specific dates of liabilities and reconciliations
- Liabilities
- Bank balance information for reconciliations to trust liabilities
- Interest-bearing accounts.

When the audit is finished, the results of the audit will be reviewed by the broker. In the event that there are any serious discrepancies, the investigator will send a comprehensive report to the Division of Real Estate issued as a formal complaint. Minor discrepancies may cause a notice of noncompliance to be issued or a fine to be levied. Complaints submitted regarding serious discrepancies will be reviewed by the Florida Real Estate Commission. In the event that this occurs, there is a disciplinary process that is followed. The complaint is filed, an investigation is conducted, a panel to review probable cause is formed, a formal complaint is made and then either an informal conference or a formal hearing will take place. The Florida Real Estate Commission will issue its final order, and at that point the broker will be allowed to issue an appeal if he/she wishes to do so. The full statute under Florida law can be found under Chapters 455 and 457.

Penalties for such violations include:

- Denial of a license application
- Refusal to renew a license
- Suspension of a license for up to 10 years
- License revocation
- A citation
- A fine of $5,000 or less
- Probation through the Florida Real Estate Commission
- A notice of noncompliance for first-time offenders concerning minor violations, or a disciplinary letter of reprimand that will stay in the licensee's file indefinitely.

Serious infractions will be turned over to a Florida court to be managed judicially. Such repercussions can include a second-degree misdemeanor with a fine of $500 or less and/or jail time of no more than 60 days. A first-degree misdemeanor will result in fines of $1,000 or less and/or jail time not to exceed one year. Civil penalties include being sued in civil court . The Department of Business and Professional Regulations may also level a fine of up to $5,000 against the licensee for violations, per Florida statute Chapter 455.

Brokers are not allowed to perform appraisals on properties, with the exception of brokers who hold a Florida State appraiser's license. With that in mind, brokers do arrange to have appraisals done during purchases and sales of properties. Brokers may conduct comparative market analyses which are unofficial and do not hold an actual value for the property, but can help with listing and reaching a reasonable listing price.

Brokers still need to be familiar with appraisals and their components. Understanding cost, price and value is a good place to start. Appraisers will also value a property. Properties are assigned value based on:

- Investment value
- Assessed value
- Liquidation value
- Salvage value
- Insurable value, or
- Market value.

Appraisers use a set of principles when valuing a property. Those principles include

- Supply and demand
- Principle of anticipation
- Principle of substitution
- Principle of increasing and decreasing returns
- Principle of conformity
- External economies and dis economies, highest and best use as though vacant, and highest and best use as improved.

When an appraiser reviews a property for a broker, seller or buyer he/she will conduct a preliminary analysis, follow the process of highest- and best-use analysis, estimate the value of the land, apply the three approaches to valuation, review reconciliation and report the value placed on the property. The final report will be provided to the customer.

Much like an appraisal, brokers may choose to compose a comparative market analysis for their clients. A comparative market analysis must contain the following information:

- The name and address of the property owners
- A full legal description of the property
- The dimensions of the lot
- The number and types of rooms for structures on the property as well as the overall square footage
- The date and type of construction that is located on the property
- Information on the properties and neighborhood including things such as schools, parks, recreational facilities, etc.
- Current property tax information
- The amount of any existing mortgages on the property
- The average cost of utility bills for the property
- Any appliances that will be included in the purchase price
- The current zoning for the property—especially important when doing an analysis on a vacant lot
- Personal property and/or fixtures that will be included in the purchase price
- Any environmental hazards.

As you compare properties you will consider

- Location
- Lot size/shape
- Landscaping
- Construction quality
- Style/design
- Chronological age of the property
- Square footage

- Heating and cooling systems
- Total number of rooms
- Kitchen size and features
- Exterior and interior condition
- Garage, if the property has one, and
- Any other relevant improvements such as swimming pools, spas or finished basements.

All of that information is used to review properties in the area that are comparable to the property you're reviewing.

As a broker you conduct business valuations anytime that you assess, market or sell a business for an individual or entity. The point of this valuation is to determine the property's value based not only on the physical property but also on the particulars of what that business may be worth. Business valuations may be done

- Regarding the sale or purchase of a business
- In order to allocate specific assets
- For the purpose of reporting financially
- When developing a buy/sell agreement
- When liquidating a business
- As part of a prenuptial agreement or divorce proceeding
- In regard to an inheritance or taxes on an estate
- Anytime eminent domain takes place
- When developing employee benefit plans, or
- When establishing a value for insuring the property.

When determining the value of a property you must first:

- Determine the type of property which you are conducting the assessment for
- Decide on a date for the valuation which will establish the value as of that specific date
- Collect all the necessary data required in order to do the analysis
- Analyze the data you've collected
- Make a final estimate of the value based on the findings
- Prepare an evaluation report, and

- Present your evaluation to the property owner.

The business valuation report should include:

- The purpose for the valuation being conducted
- An outline and definition of the value that's been estimated
- An outline of the process used to evaluate the business
- The date on which the value estimate is effective
- A summary of facts
- A statement summarizing the conclusions that were reached
- A list of assumptions and/or limiting conditions, and
- Any supporting data such as maps.

Real estate agents handle four types of contracts:

- Sale and purchase contracts

  A sale and purchase contract refers to any contract that is between two parties, one of which represents a buyer and the other representing the seller in a purchase and sale of real property

- Listing agreements

  Listing agreements are between a broker and a seller, who is an employee, in order for the seller to perform specific real estate services.

- Buyer broker agreements

A buyer broker agreement is an employment agreement prepared between a broker and a buyer to execute real estate services.

- Options contracts.

An options contract is between a potential seller and a potential buyer. The seller provides the potential buyer with options granting him/her rights based on certain terms and conditions for the potential buyer to purchase the property.

As a broker it will be incredibly important that you have a comprehensive understanding of local state and government laws pertaining to real estate. You should also have a comprehensive understanding of the financing options potentially available to prospective buyers. As a real estate associate, part of your job will be walking customers through the process of buying, selling or leasing real estate. This may include counseling your clients on the steps to take or advising them about who to talk to regarding the financing and/or insuring of their property.

As a broker, your responsibility will be to ensure that closings are conducted properly. It's important to be able to help buyers and sellers come to an agreement, complete all the necessary documents correctly and finalize the sale or purchase. Closings occur once property is transferred from a seller to a buyer with the transfer of the property's title. When closing documents are signed, you will inform the MLS that the property is under contract.

The sale and purchase agreement should include the:

- Date and location of closing
- Purchase price of the property
- Legal description of the property
- Quality of the title
- Method by which the title's quality has been insured
- Financing information, if it was required for the purchase
- Kind of deed that is being conveyed
- Exclusion of any real property, and
- Inclusion of any personal property.

Properties being purchased will go through an appraisal to ensure financing. Additionally, inspections will be done to check for termites, mold and construction quality. When the closing commences, any money that will be paid between the buyer and seller as either a shared financial amount or an old financial amount will be provided. In some events, proration will also be applied.

As a real estate broker, not only will you handle property management, sales and purchasing, but you will also delve into the world of real estate investments. To perform this duty, you will need to understand what real estate investment is comprised of. You must understand the types of property, whether residential or non-residential; understand the investment before and after any taxes that apply to it and be able to judge the market and the investment being made.

One of the first things you will do is perform a client evaluation. Before you can look for new properties to buy you need to understand:

- What your client currently holds in assets and liabilities
- What kind of investment your client is looking for
- The amount of capital available for the investment
- Whether your client has the funding up front or will require financing
- The financing that's available in the time that will be available to manage those investments.

Any investment carries a certain level of inherent risk. Knowing the property and having all of its information is important, as the unknowns of any given property can inherently cause more risk. Anytime you consider managing an investment you need to understand that it is quite an undertaking. If a client is managing his/her own property, this can reduce the overall expense versus having a broker or other financial individual managing it for them. Management fees are one of the largest expenses pertaining to investment properties and their overall operating expenses. Property management fees or investment management fees can cost between 10% and 50% of what the property earns.

The larger the investment, the larger the risk. Understanding these risks and being able to articulate to your client the risks that they're taking will be an important part of your job. Ultimately, it's about understanding the dynamics of investment risks. When it comes to risk and investment, it's important to consider business risks, financial risks and capital risks. If an individual invests into a property, and then that property generates no return or costs a property owner more then what it generates, that is a loss to the property owner, which ultimately makes it a bad investment.

Understanding the market is important. If the market is poor, the investment will ultimately flounder. Ensuring that your investment property and the business of that property are purchased and run in a location that is beneficial to that business also plays a large role. An alternative to investing in property can be stocks and bonds that you purchase towards a company, rather than buying a property outright. Stocks and bonds can offer some benefits, such as not having the operating expenses of owning a real estate investment. Rather, you're investing in a business that is already established. At the same time, if the value of a business that you own stock in drops, so does the overall value of your investment.

Some clients may purchase, or already own a property, that they choose to rent or lease residentially or commercially as their investment. If the property is already owned outright, any income a client earns off that property is a financial gain, and any lost commonly pertains to the upkeep, maintenance, repairs or remodeling of their property.

Clients who have a loan or mortgage on an investment property will earn money by charging a rent or lease in an amount that is higher than what they pay out in their personal mortgage and insurance on that property. For example, if an individual has a property whose mortgage is $300 a month and his/her insurance for that property is $150 a month, the individual pays out $450 a month for owning that property. To make a profit, the property owner would rent or lease that property for an amount higher than $450. When calculating the return you are looking for on your investment, you want to consider a portion of that profit that can be set aside for any damages or repairs needed by the property as well. So, a property owner may rent a three-bedroom, two-bathroom rental property for $1,000 a month. $450 of that $1,000 covers the mortgage and insurance. $550 is then left to be divided between property maintenance, property taxes and profit.

Whether you're dealing with a commercial property or a residential property, the owner will have some level of expense for its maintenance and/or operating expenses, as well as property taxes. In the event that a property becomes vacant, or the business closes, property owners need to be prepared to handle the cost of still maintaining that investment.

So overall when considering an investment property, it is important for you and your clients to be aware of the costs that property may have and the earnings it can generate. Start by calculating the potential gross income of an investment property and determine how much income a given property can generate under the best-case scenario. From there you will calculate the effective gross income of an investment property, and the net operating income. This information will be used to decide on a property's overall investment value.

For example, you would calculate the potential gross income, the expense of any vacancies or collections, calculate the effective gross income of the property and deduct from that the operating expenses. Those expenses include repairs, real estate taxes, property insurance, utilities for the property and the cost of having the property maintained.

Once you understand the total expenses of an investment property, you can deduct those expenses to determine what the property's net operating income will be. With these numbers you can estimate the overall annual earnings and losses the property will most likely experience. The expenses of the property should never cost more than what a property can generate. If they do, you are looking at a bad investment.

As a broker, you will organize this information and present it in the most straightforward way to help prospective buyers and clients make the best choices on a real estate investment.

As a broker you'll be managing properties for investment and conducting property management for individual clients. In some cases, you may even be the owner-manager of a property or multiple properties. This responsibility may include but is not limited to managing rental properties or overseeing and managing a business for the property owner.

Other responsibilities you will have as a broker include:

- Showing properties that you're managing
- Helping prospective tenants complete applications
- Reviewing applications for leasing or renting properties
- Preparing and executing leases
- Collecting deposits and rents
- Conducting routine inspections
- Facilitating repairs when they're needed
- Training or supervising staff
- Handling a property's bookkeeping
- Inspecting and maintaining building systems like heat and air
- Facilitating the landlord-tenant relationship
- Knowing and understanding the layout and design
- Marketing and advertising properties

- Staying current on community issues, and
- Knowing the local, state, and federal laws that apply to the properties you are managing.

Ensuring that the properties you manage have good-quality tenants is important. Establishing tenant policies and ensuring that leases are properly executed is your responsibility. A lease should include:

- The name of the landlord
- The name of the tenant(s)
- A legal description of the property that's being leased
- The terms and conditions for that lease
- The rental amount
- Property usage
- The rights and responsibilities of the landlord and/or property manager, and
- The rights and responsibilities of the person renting the property.

There are a variety of leases that property managers need to understand and now how to execute. Those include:

- A fixed lease
- Graduated lease
- Ground lease
- Net lease
- Percentage lease, and
- A gross lease.

As a property manager, you will also be required to:

- Maintain the physical integrity of the property
- Ensure that all functions of the property are performing properly
- Ensure that housekeeping is done to maintain the cleanliness and upkeep of the property, and
- Ensure the property is marketable.

Properties come in all shapes, sizes and locations. To that end, it's important to make sure that:

- Maintenance is conducted
- Inspections to the property are done on a routine schedule
- Bookkeeping is kept current and legible
- Proper record-keeping of inspections and maintenance are well maintained
- Copies of all executed leases and any notices to tenants are kept on file, and
- All city and county licensing and other requirements are kept current.

In summary, as a broker you must know local, state and federal laws. You'll be responsible for ensuring that your business, the sales associates and employees who work for you, and your clients follow the law while conducting real estate business. Knowing your local codes, zoning, environmental and wetland restrictions, and being able to navigate within those parameters while conducting business will be a priority. Ultimately, you will be responsible for the confidentiality and accountability for your business and your business associates. You must keep meticulous records on all your business dealings, finances, contracts, client and prospective client information.

It will be your responsibility to ensure that your business is working within the Florida Real Estate Commission, and Department of Business and Professional Regulations' standards of conduct. Losing your license or having it suspended affects everyone working under you as a broker. Making sure that things are done to the codes, bylaws and other standards expected of you will ensure that you and those you supervise can all thrive and succeed.

# Chapter 9: Real Estate Math

Real estate math is something that you may not think too much about, but it is something you will deal with on a daily basis and is an important component in your career. When it comes to real estate math, you will be responsible for:

- Bookkeeping in your office
- Managing an escrow account
- Working out commissions and closing costs
- Calculating proration
- Completing comparative market analyses
- Calculating appreciation, equity and depreciation
- Calculating actual profit, principle payment amounts, interest rates, taxable income, liquidated damages, loan to value ratios and so on.

Below are some key formulas and mathematic breakdowns that will be beneficial to you in the real estate field.

## Percentage to Decimal Conversions

½% = 0.005

1% = 0.01

10% = 0.10

100% = 1.00

125% = 1.25

## Square Footage to Acreage Conversions

- There are 43,560 square feet (sq. ft.) per acre
- Square footage of a rectangle = base × height
- Square feet to acres = 43,560 square feet × the number of acres
- Acres to square feet = number of acres × 43,560 square feet

## Mathematic Formulas

- Depreciation value of the property = reproduction cost – depreciation + site value
- Effective gross income = potential gross income – vacancy & collections
- Net operating income = effective gross income – operating expenses
- Profit = sales price – acquisition price
- Percentage of profits = profit ÷ acquisition price
- Monthly rate of change = percentage of profit ÷ the number of months of ownership
- Multiplier = value ÷ monthly rent
- Income capitalization amount = net operating income ÷ capitalization rate × value
- Residual land value = net operating income ÷ capitalization rate – cost of construction
- Taxable income = net operating income + reserves – mortgage interest – depreciation

## Calculating Amortization

1. Loan amount × annual interest rate = annual interest rate
2. Annual interest rate ÷ 12 months = monthly interest
3. Mortgage payment (principal + interest) – monthly interest = principle portion
4. Principle loan balance of loan – principle portion of payment = new loan balance

## Calculating Commission

1. Net price + closing costs = total to net
2. Total to net – commission percentage = broker's commission

## Cost Depreciation Approach

1. Reproduction cost ÷ economic life × effective age = total depreciation
2. Reproduction cost – total depreciation + land value = depreciated value of the property

# Sales Associates Practice Test 1

1. Before taking the Florida Real Estate Licensing Exam for Sales Associates, you must first pass a ____-hour pre-licensing education course.
    a. 63
    b. 14
    c. 72
    d. 16

2. A passing score for the sales associate pre-licensing education course is ____ or higher.
    a. 70%
    b. 80%
    c. 75%
    d. 85%

3. What agency must approve and certify a pre-licensing education course in order for it to meet the real estate education requirements?
    a. The Better Business Bureau
    b. The Florida Real Estate Commission
    c. The Department of Business and Professional Regulation
    d. The Florida Department of Education

4. The State of Florida allows individuals to take pre-licensing courses in a ____ or ____ setting so long as the course is approved through the Florida Real Estate Commission.
    a. Group or individual
    b. Computer-enabled or paper-based
    c. College or trade school
    d. Classroom or online

5. In the State of Florida, you are required to be at least ____ years of age in order to be eligible to take the real estate licensing exam.
    a. 18
    b. 16
    c. 21
    d. 25

6. Which of the following tasks must you complete in order to satisfy the pre-licensing education course requirements so that you can move on to the state exam?
    a. You must be present for at least half of the required course hours in a classroom
    b. You must attend the full number of required classroom hours
    c. You must pass the pre-licensing end-of-course exam
    d. You must attend the required class hours and pass the course exam at the end

7. How long does your certificate of completion remain valid after you pass your real estate pre-licensing course in Florida?
    a. 12 months
    b. 18 months
    c. 24 months
    d. 36 months

8. Which of the following documents are you required to obtain in order to prove that you have passed your pre-licensing exam?
    a. A Florida Real Estate License
    b. A certificate of completion for your pre-licensing course
    c. A college degree from an accredited university
    d. An official copy of your college transcripts

9. Which of the following individuals are not required to fulfill the pre-licensing education course requirements before taking their Florida Real Estate Licensing Exam?
    a. Lawyers who have graduated law school, taken and passed the Florida Bar Exam and have a valid Florida Bar card to practice law in the State of Florida
    b. Property managers who work in an apartment complex or condominium in Florida and regularly rent apartments or condos to tenants
    c. A timeshare sales associate who manages timeshare properties in the State of Florida and is familiar with the state's practices and procedures
    d. An individual who is educated, qualified and licensed as an appraiser in Florida

10. If you have a bachelor's degree or higher with a focus on real estate and have taken at least as many course hours as Florida requires, which of the following documents are you permitted to provide in order to satisfy the pre-licensing education requirements?
    a. A Florida college master's degree in real estate
    b. A college referral letter from one or more professors
    c. An official copy of college transcripts
    d. A college course list

11. Which of the following organizations schedules and conducts the real estate licensing exam in Florida?
    a. The Florida Department of Business and Professional Regulation
    b. The Florida Real Estate Commission
    c. Pearson VUE
    d. The National Association of Realtors

12. Once you have successfully completed your pre-licensing education course, which of the following is the first step that you will need to take in the application process to take the Florida Real Estate Licensing Exam?
    a. Fill out an application
    b. Pay the licensing fee
    c. Pay the exam fee
    d. Take the state exam

13. The application fee for the Florida Real Estate Commission Application for Sales Associates is:
    a. $91.75
    b. $83.75
    c. $72.75
    d. $61.75

14. You can pay your application fee in all of the following ways, except:
    a. By personal check
    b. By money order
    c. By credit card
    d. Through PayPal

15. Digital fingerprinting is part of the ____ during the application process and is a requirement before you can take your real estate exam.
    a. Credit check
    b. Identification
    c. Background check
    d. Licensing

16. Which of the following *must* be included with your application in order for the application to be processed?
    a. Digital fingerprints
    b. A copy of your driver's license
    c. College transcripts
    d. A copy of your birth certificate

17. Digital fingerprints should be taken at least how many days prior to submitting your exam application?
    a. 3 days
    b. 5 days
    c. 7 days
    d. 14 days

18. An incomplete exam application will result in which of the following actions?
    a. Suspension
    b. Expiration
    c. Rejection
    d. Deactivation

19. What individuals or entities are responsible for performing digital fingerprinting in the State of Florida?
    a. The Florida Licensing Board
    b. Pearson VUE
    c. The Florida Department of Law Enforcement
    d. A Live Scan vendor

20. Which type of background check is used when applying for a real estate license?
    a. A Level 2 background check
    b. A complete criminal history background check
    c. An FBI background check
    d. A pre-employment background check

21. You *must* schedule an appointment in order to do which of the following activities?
    a. Submit your application to the Department of Business and Professional Regulation
    b. Have your fingerprints taken by a certified Live Scan vendor
    c. Take a pre-licensing education course
    d. Provide proof of your pre-licensing course completion

22. A Level 2 background check includes what government agencies?
    a. City, county and state agencies
    b. State, federal and international agencies
    c. Local, state and federal agencies
    d. Local police departments

23. All of the following forms of identification are examples of a primary ID except:
    a. A valid military ID card
    b. A valid driver's license
    c. A DOD Common Access Card
    d. A certified copy of a birth certificate

24. Which of the following agencies is the first to receive the results from a background check?
    a. The Florida Department of Law Enforcement
    b. The Florida Department of Business and Professional Regulation
    c. The Florida Real Estate Commission
    d. The Florida Division of Real Estate

25. You will not be allowed to have your digital fingerprints taken:
    a. If your forms of ID do not match
    b. If you have a photo ID
    c. If you provide a primary form of ID
    d. If you provide a secondary form of ID

26. The cost to have your Live Scan digital fingerprints taken can differ from vendor to vendor, but the price usually ranges between:
    a. $10 and $20
    b. $30 and $50
    c. $40 and $90
    d. $75 and $100

27. How long do your digital fingerprints stay on file with the Florida Department of Law Enforcement once you have had them taken for your state licensing exam?
    a. 30 days
    b. 45 days
    c. 3 months
    d. 6 months

28. If you do not submit your application for the Florida Real Estate Licensing Exam within six months of ________, you will have to repeat this action before your application can be processed.
    a. Having your digital fingerprints taken
    b. Completing your pre-licensing course
    c. Submitting your licensing exam application
    d. Paying the exam fees

29. In which of the following locations will you take your real estate licensing exam?
    a. A Pearson VUE testing center
    b. The Florida Real Estate Commissioner's office
    c. A Prometric testing center
    d. The Florida Department of Law Enforcement office

30. Individuals can register for the state real estate licensing exam with Pearson VUE in all of the following ways except:
    a. Over the phone
    b. Online
    c. In person
    d. Both A and B

31. The cost to take the Florida Real Estate Licensing Exam is ____ each time you take it.
    a. $22.75
    b. $36.75
    c. $47.75
    d. $82.75

32. You can reschedule or cancel your real estate licensing exam appointment, without penalty, up to:
    a. 24 hours before your scheduled exam
    b. 48 hours before your scheduled exam
    c. 96 hours before your scheduled exam
    d. 2 weeks before your scheduled exam

33. You forfeit your right to a full refund of your licensing exam fee if you ____ on the day of your testing appointment.
    a. Are absent
    b. Arrive after the exam start time
    c. Cancel before the testing day
    d. Both A and B

34. In the event that you miss your testing appointment, there are a few reasons that may warrant consideration and be excused, but they will require you to provide:
    a. Supporting documents
    b. A phone call
    c. Your written notice
    d. Both B and C

35. In order to check in for your real estate licensing exam, you are asked to arrive ____ at the Pearson VUE testing facility.
    a. On time
    b. 30 minutes before your appointment
    c. 15 minutes before your appointment
    d. 45 minutes before your appointment

36. Cell phones and purses are considered personal items and should be:
    a. Kept in plain sight
    b. Kept with you at all times
    c. Left in the locker provided by the testing facility
    d. Stored under your desk during testing

37. Your real estate licensing exam will be administered in which of the following formats?
    a. A test booklet and answer sheet
    b. A textbook and essay question
    c. With a pen and paper
    d. Using a testing facility computer

38. You will be given roughly ____ to familiarize yourself with the computer, learn how the test program operates and ask any operational or technical questions.
    a. 5 minutes
    b. 15 minutes
    c. 25 minutes
    d. 30 minutes

39. Test administrators are allowed to answer only questions regarding:
    a. The computer and program
    b. Leaving the testing room
    c. The exam and contents
    d. When you are allowed to begin

40. How much time are you allotted to complete the real estate licensing exam?
   a. An hour and a half
   b. Two and a half hours
   c. Three and a half hours
   d. Four and a half hours

41. How many multiple-choice questions are on the Florida Real Estate Licensing Exam?
   a. 40
   b. 80
   c. 100
   d. 400

42. You must score a minimum of ____/____ to pass the real estate exam.
   a. 70/100
   b. 90/120
   c. 175/200
   d. 75/100

43. Which of the following is a description of an adjustable mortgage rate?
   a. A mortgage loan that has a fluctuating interest rate
   b. A mortgage loan that has a set interest rate
   c. A mortgage loan that allows the interest to be paid up front
   d. A mortgage loan that is interest-free with payment amounts that fluctuate

44. When a licensed individual determines the value of a property and generates an official report of his/her findings, these findings are called:
    a. A comparative market analysis
    b. An appraisal
    c. A market valuation
    d. A binding arbitration

45. When a loan payment is due that is much larger than the usual monthly payment, this payment is known as:
    a. A down payment
    b. An escrow
    c. A balloon payment
    d. An earnest money deposit

46. Mark sells his home for $327,900. His broker, Sally, gets a commission of 9% from the sale. How much is Sally's commission?
    a. $29,511.00
    b. $298,686.57
    c. $328,227.00
    d. $32,790.00

47. The Tango Bar and Grill downtown sells for $1,530,000; closing costs are $15,300. Davis, the broker who sold the property, gets an 11% commission. How much is Davis' commission?
    a. $1,545,300.00
    b. $169,983.00
    c. $1,715,283.00
    d. $1,375,317.00

48. Mara sells her beach house for $824,600; the closing costs are $8,246. The buyer is paying half of the closing costs. Mara's broker, Sam, is earning a 7% commission from the sale. How much is Sam's commission?

   a. $4,123.00
   b. $770,712.39
   c. $58,010.61
   d. $868,733.61

49. Michael sells his ski lodge in the Alps for $2,630,300; the closing costs are $26,303. Michael's broker, Kelly, is earning a 30% commission from the sale. How much is Kelly's commission for this sale?

   a. $2,656,603.00
   b. $3,449,683.90
   c. $1,857,522.10
   d. $796,980.90

50. Ella is putting in flower beds to add curb appeal to her property. The rectangular flower beds are six inches wide and six feet long. What is the area of each of Ella's flowerbeds?

   a. 6 square feet
   b. 3 square feet
   c. 2 square feet
   d. 12 square feet

51. A townhouse was purchased with a down payment of $10,000 and a mortgage of $350,000 at an interest rate of 5% for a 30-year term. The monthly payments are $1,500. What is the loan-to-value ratio?

   a. 2.86 %
   b. 2.78 %
   c. 91.4 %
   d. 97.2 %

Mtg ÷ SP
350.000/360.000

52. A dance studio rents for $30 per square foot with an index of 2.5. The index increases to 3.0. What is the adjustable rental rate?
   a. $36
   b. $26
   c. $46
   d. $56

53. A warehouse in Newtown rents for $12.20 per square foot with an index of 1.3. The index increases to 2.7. What is the adjustable rental rate?
   a. $24.48
   b. $25.34
   c. $26.28
   d. $27.18

54. A club downtown rents for $22 a square foot with an index of 3.4. The index increases to 4.7. What is the adjustable rental rate?
   a. $20.36
   b. $25.36
   c. $30.41
   d. $35.36

55. A high-rise in midtown rents for $765 a square foot with an index of 46.75. The index increases to 72.94. What is the adjustable rental rate?
   a. $119.69
   b. $46.75
   c. $3,409.95
   d. $1,193.56

56. Which legal term refers to a property owner who does not live on the property and usually employs a property manager to take care of the property's day-to-day needs?
    a. Landlord
    b. Absentee owner
    c. Investment manager
    d. Commingling

57. An acceleration clause refers to what in a loan contract?
    a. A legal clause in a loan contract that accelerates the timeline in which the loan is repaid
    b. A legal clause found in loan contracts that shortens the time the property spends in escrow
    c. A legal clause that binds the contracted party.
    d. A legal clause in a loan contract that speeds up the time frame in which closing is completed

58. The legal term that refers to a property's value being used to calculate the taxes that are owed on the property is:
    a. Arbitration
    b. Capital gain
    c. High and best use
    d. Ad valorem

59. What is the legal term that refers to parties bringing a legal matter before a judge alone rather than in front of a jury, presenting their sides and evidence to the judge, and the judge then making a final ruling?
    a. Arbitration
    b. Summary judgment
    c. Citation
    d. Culpable negligence

60. The illegal action of using fear to pressure an individual or entity into selling property, usually at a loss, and then reselling that property for a substantial profit is known as:
    a. Capital gains
    b. Blockbusting
    c. Culpable negligence
    d. Encroachment

61. Local government uses ______ to ensure that new construction and remodels to existing properties are done in a standardized way to ensure the overall safety of the property.
    a. Further assurance
    b. Property reports
    c. Building codes
    d. Buffer zones

62. Local government requires that individuals and entities acquire a ____ in order to legally build new construction, renovate, and demolish both commercial and residential properties.
    a. Citation
    b. Certificate of occupancy
    c. Contract
    d. Building permit

63. What is a constructive notice?
   a. A legal action in which a notice is placed in a newspaper, and possibly other public forums, to inform of legal action that is being taken when the individual or party the action is taken against cannot be reached personally
   b. A legal notice in which an individual conducts an evaluation of a property and formulates a report outlining the property's pros and cons in a constructive and beneficial way
   c. A legal notice placed on the door of a property to inform the inhabitants that the property will be demolished and telling them of the time they are allotted to vacate the property
   d. A legal notice that is placed in clear view to inform the public that local government permission has been given to allow construction or remodeling

64. A ______ is a legally binding written agreement between parties, outlining the terms of a deal, the stipulations in the event that it is broken and other miscellaneous points that the parties would like included.
   a. Deed
   b. Contract
   c. Title
   d. Bond

65. What is the legal term that refers to a real estate agent neglecting a client or customer to the extent that it causes financial damage?
   a. Citation
   b. Depreciation
   c. Culpable negligence
   d. Disintermediation

66. What is the legal term for a piece of a property belonging to one party that is legally allowed to be used by another party, generally for the purpose of reaching their own property that does not otherwise have an access point?
    a. Escrow
    b. Lien
    c. Encasement
    d. Easement

67. In a mortgage contract, a clause that requires payment in full if a mortgage has a balance at the time a property is sold is called:
    a. Due-on-sale clause
    b. Appreciation clause
    c. Exculpatory clause
    d. Granting clause

68. ______ allows local, state or federal government to take private property (compensating the property owner at fair market value) from an individual or party and repurpose that property for public use.
    a. Property seizure
    b. Eminent domain
    c. Foreclosure
    d. Forfeiture

69. When an individual trespasses on a neighboring property, this illegal activity is known as:
    a. Disintermediation
    b. Intermediary
    c. Encroachment
    d. Nolo contendere

70. What is the term for a state law that gives ownership of a property to the state when a resident of that state dies with no will and no next of kin?
    a. Exempt property
    b. Exculpatory
    c. Eminent domain
    d. Escheat

71. A legal written lease that has a set date to commence and a set date to discontinue is known as:
    a. Estate for years
    b. Deed in lieu of foreclosure
    c. Chain of title
    d. Consent to transition

72. Which term refers to a property that is legally exempt from having the value of its taxes determined by the value of the property?
    a. Freehold estate
    b. Exempt property
    c. Further assurance
    d. Going-concern value

73. Which of the terms describes a legal document that ensures a property title is produced "free and clear"?
    a. Guarantee
    b. Guardian's deed
    c. Further assurance
    d. Granting clause

74. Which of the following terms correctly refers to individuals who have severe restrictions in their ability to complete everyday tasks because of a mental or physical deficit?
    a. Incompetent party
    b. Grantor status
    c. Intermediary
    d. Handicap status

75. What is the legal term that refers to laws that are put in place for the health and well-being of the community?
    a. Health ordinance
    b. Certificate of occupancy
    c. Legally sufficient
    d. Public accommodations

76. Which of the following appropriately describes the law that protects surviving spouses, minor children and unmarried children from losing their home when the head of household dies?
    a. Florida Fair Housing Law
    b. Homestead Law
    c. Green Belt Law
    d. Fair Housing Act of 1968

77. Which of the following terms correctly describes when a judge determines who is legally entitled to funds pertaining to a real estate matter?
    a. Summary judgment
    b. Settlement
    c. Interpleader
    d. Legally sufficient

78. Which of the following terms is used to describe a lender's or creditor's legal claim to personal property, primarily when the personal property in question is used as collateral?
    a. Liabilities
    b. Acquisitions
    c. Entitlement
    d. Lien

79. Which of the following terms describes a sum charged to an individual, party or entity for breaking a contract before the conditions are met?
    a. Liquidated damages
    b. Due-on-sale clause
    c. Good-faith doubt
    d. Gross rent multiplier

80. Which of the following terms refers to being informed of legal action?
    a. Ad valorem
    b. Lis pendens
    c. Declaration
    d. Interpleader

81. The Marketable Record Title Act (Florida Statutes, Chapter 712) is responsible for doing which of the following?
    a. Making titles for marketable properties readily available
    b. Limiting the terms of a mortgage to 15 years
    c. Placing a 30-year limit on title matter defects
    d. Both A and B

82. Which of the following terms refers to a non-biased third party helping two or more parties come to an agreement regarding a legal matter?
    a. Negotiation
    b. Summary judgment
    c. Arbitration
    d. Mediation

83. Which of the following terms means the same as "no contest"?
    a. Nolo contendere
    b. Withstand
    c. Contendere
    d. Counteracted

84. Which of the following terms describes the ability to legally continue the preexisting use of a property for a purpose the area it resides in is no longer zoned for?
    a. Specialty property
    b. Nonconforming use
    c. Exempt property
    d. Personal representative's deed

85. Which of the following terms is the correct word to describe a legal document that shows a debt or multiple debts that are owed?
    a. Title
    b. Receipt
    c. Note
    d. Conveyance

86. What is police power?
    a. Laws that allow communities to have law enforcement and enact laws
    b. The legal right to control the situation
    c. Laws that protect the welfare of one individual
    d. A set of laws made for the health, safety and welfare of the public

87. What is the legal term for a justifiable reason to prosecute?
    a. Probable cause
    b. Fiduciary
    c. Speculation
    d. Probate

88. Which of the following terms refers to the illegal act of refusing funding to those from specific areas or demographics?
    a. Benchmark
    b. Redlining
    c. Blockbusting
    d. Appropriation

89. What is the correct term for the ability to use a property for a purpose that is generally against a zoning law or other such laws?
    a. Exempt property
    b. Allowances
    c. Special exception
    d. Exclusion

90. Which term refers to the legal need to have specific matters put in writing in order for those terms or agreements to be enforced?

   a. Statute of limitations
   b. Contract
   c. Lease
   d. Statute of frauds

91. Which of the following terms refers to a limit on the amount of time an individual, group or entity has to seek legal action to resolve a matter?

   a. Statute of limitations
   b. Due process
   c. Terms of lease
   d. Subpoena

92. Which of the following terms accurately represents the legal summons and requirement to appear before a court of law?

   a. Testament
   b. Subpoena
   c. Contract
   d. Deed

93. Which of the following terms refers to the inability to seek out legal action on a given matter?

   a. Irrelevant
   b. Invalid
   c. Unenforceable
   d. Unappreciated

94. Which of the following terms refers to the legal requirements being met in regard to a contract?
    a. Profitable
    b. Executed
    c. Supported
    d. Valid

95. What does it mean if a contract or license is void?
    a. It is not legally enforceable
    b. It is valid and enforced
    c. It is temporarily not to be used
    d. Both B and C

96. Title 32, Chapter 475.02 of the Florida statutes outlines the responsibilities of which agency?
    a. The Division of Real Estate
    b. The Florida Real Estate Commission
    c. The Department of Business and Professional Regulation
    d. The National Association of Realtors

97. Title 32, Chapter 475.021 outlines the services provided by which agency?
    a. The Florida Real Estate Commission
    b. The Florida Department of Business and Professional Regulation
    c. The Division of Real Estate
    d. The Division of Professional Development

98. Under Florida law, what is the purpose of the Florida Real Estate Commission Education and Research Foundation?
   a. Educational expansion
   b. Evolving continued education
   c. Licensing and exams
   d. Both A and B

99. Which entity is responsible for the rules, requirements and laws pertaining to the education and licensing of real estate agents?
   a. The Florida Real Estate Commission
   b. The Division of Real Estate
   c. The Better Business Bureau
   d. The Department of Business and Professional Regulation

100. Under Title 32, Chapter 475.125 of the Florida statutes, the Florida Real Estate Commission and the Florida Department of Business and Professional Regulation are responsible for the ____ associated with education, examination, licensing and continued education.
   a. Valuations
   b. Fees
   c. Reading materials
   d. Advertising

# Answers – Sales Associates Practice Test 1

1. Answer: a. 63
   Individuals who wish to take the Florida Real Estate Licensing Exam for Sales Associates must first complete a 63-hour pre-licensing course. You must fulfill the full 63 hours of instruction requirement, take the final pre-licensing course exam at the end of the course and pass that exam with a score of 75% or higher in order to be permitted to move on to the application process for the Florida Real Estate Licensing Exam.

2. Answer: c. 75%
   Individuals who take the real estate pre-licensing education course must take the exam at the end of the course, pass with 75% or higher and collect the certificate of completion in order to be able to take the state licensing exam.

3. Answer: b. The Florida Real Estate Commission
   In order for a sales associate pre-licensing education course to meet the pre-licensing education requirements for the Florida Real Estate Exam, the course must be certified and approved by the Florida Real Estate Commission.

4. Answer: d. Classroom or online
   The State of Florida and the Florida Real Estate Commission have certified an array of courses and various qualified locations for individuals to take real estate pre-licensing education courses. There are courses that are approved for on-site classroom instruction and a variety of online programs, many of which allow you to set your own pace. It is your responsibility to ensure that the course you choose is approved by the Florida Real Estate Commission, regardless of the setting.

5. Answer: a. 18
   The State of Florida mandates that an individual be at least 18 years of age in order to qualify to take the Florida Real Estate Licensing Exam. Additionally, most programs require you to be at least 18 years old to take the pre-licensing education courses, though there are some select allowances made for some individuals under 18.

6. Answer: d. You must attend the required class hours and pass the course exam at the end
   In order to apply to take the Florida Real Estate Licensing Exam for Sales Associates, you must meet pre-qualification requirements. The pre-licensing education requirement involves completing a 63-hour pre-licensing instruction and education course. At the end of the pre-licensing education course, you must successfully pass the course exam with a score of 75% or higher. Individuals must collect their certification of completion at the end of the course. This will be needed as you advance into the application and state testing phases. Then you will move on to the exam application process.

7. Answer: c. 24 months
   After you have successfully completed the pre-licensing education course for real estate sales associates, you will collect your certificate of completion. That certificate is valid for 24 months, or two years, from the date on the document. If you do not take and/or pass the Florida Real Estate Licensing Exam for Sales Associates before that two-year window is over, you will be required to pay for and retake the pre-licensing education course.

8. Answer: b. A certificate of completion for your pre-licensing course
   Each individual is required to complete a real estate pre-licensing course for sales associates, pass the end-of-course exam and collect the certificate of completion at the end of the course. This certificate will be relevant

when applying for the Florida Real Estate Licensing Exam for Sales Associates.

9. Answer: a. Lawyers who have graduated law school, taken and passed the Florida Bar Exam and have a valid Florida Bar card to practice law in the State of Florida.
   Individuals who have attended law school, successfully passed the Florida Bar and can legally practice law in the state of Florida with an active and current Bar card are exempt from the pre-licensing education requirements. Instead, they can submit their application to the Florida Real Estate Exam for Sales Associates with their digital fingerprints and a copy of their Florida Bar card.

10. Answer: c. An official copy of college transcripts
    Individuals who have successfully acquired their bachelor's degree with a major in real estate can be exempt from real estate sales associates' pre-licensing education requirements. Instead, those individuals can complete the application for the Florida Real Estate Exam for Sales Associates and submit it with digital fingerprints and a copy of their college transcripts.

11. Answer: c. Pearson VUE
    Florida uses Pearson VUE to schedule, administer and score professional licensing exams for the state.

12. Answer: a. Fill out an application
    In order to be approved for the Florida Real Estate Exam, the first step in the application process is to complete the application. Applications can be found online and may be printed and mailed, if so desired, instead of being electronically submitted.

13. Answer: b. $83.75
    The application fee for the Florida Real Estate Commission Application for Sales Associate License is $83.75.

14. Answer: d. Through PayPal
    You can pay with a credit card or debit card online when you fill out and submit your application to take the Florida Real Estate Licensing Exam. You can print off a paper application from the Department of Business and Professional Regulation and mail the exam fee, using either a personal check or money order, with the completed paper application. PayPal is not an acceptable form of payment.

15. Answer: c. Background check
    Having your digital fingerprints taken is part of the Level 2 background check that you are required to have as part of the application process when you are seeking to obtain your Florida Real Estate License.

16. Answer: a. Digital fingerprints
    You are required to have your digital fingerprints taken at a Live Scan facility or vendor as part of the application process for the Florida Real Estate Licensing Exam. Your personal information and digital fingerprints are used when conducting your Level 2 background check. This background check will compare your information against local and state law enforcement agencies as well as performing an FBI background check.

17. Answer: b. 5 days
    Your digital fingerprints should be taken at least five days before you submit your Florida Real Estate Licensing Exam application. If you delay too long and your digital fingerprints and background check do not come

back in time to be submitted with your application, you risk your application being rejected.

18. Answer: c. Rejection
If you submit an incomplete exam, the Florida Real Estate Commission and the Department of Business and Professional Regulation will reject your application.

19. Answer: d. A Live Scan vendor.
Digital fingerprints are taken at a Live Scan vendor that is cleared by the State of Florida.

20. Answer: a. A Level 2 background check.
Florida requires a Level 2 background check for prospective real estate associates, mainly because you will be responsible for handling other people's money and property.

21. Answer: b. Have your fingerprints taken by a certified Live Scan vendor
There are several Live Scan vendor locations in Florida, which allows you to choose the one that is most convenient for you.

22. Answer: c. Local, state and federal agencies
The Florida Real Estate Commission requires a Level 2 background check, which runs your fingerprints and personal information through the local police department database, the State of Florida database and the FBI database to check for any criminal activities. An illegal activity does not automatically exclude you from being able to become a real estate associate, but it will require further review by the real estate commission before the decision is made.

23. Answer: d. A certified copy of a birth certificate
A birth certificate is an example of a secondary form of identification. A military ID, valid driver's license and a DOD Common Access Card all have a photo, making them valid examples of a primary ID.

24. Answer: a. The Florida Department of Law Enforcement
Digital fingerprints are processed through a Live Scan vendor, and then a background check is compiled. The Florida Department of Law Enforcement receives all your information after it has been run through all necessary databases.

25. Answer: a. If your forms of ID do not match
You are required to show proper identification when you go in for your Live Scan appointment to have your digital fingerprints taken. If the appointment information you gave when you made the office visit does not match the identification you present when you go to have the prints done, you will not be allowed to have your fingerprints taken.

26. Answer: c. $40 and $90
Each Live Scan vendor is different. For that reason, the cost of the digital fingerprint scanning can vary between $40 and $90. If there is more than one Live Scan vendor near you, it may be wise to call around and see if one has a better price than another.

27. Answer: d. 6 months
The Florida Department of Law Enforcement retains your fingerprints for six months. If you have not submitted your application for your state licensing exam, have not taken the state licensing exam or have taken the state licensing exam but not passed by the time that six months is up, you may be required to start the whole process over again.

28. Answer: a. Having your digital fingerprints taken
If you do not submit your application for the real estate licensing exam within six months, you will have to repeat the digital fingerprinting step.

29. Answer: a. A Pearson VUE testing center
The Florida Real Estate Licensing Exam is administered at a Pearson VUE testing facility. There are more than 20 Pearson VUE testing centers in Florida to choose from.

30. Answer: c. In person.
You can register for the Florida Real Estate Licensing Exam by phone and online. However, Pearson VUE does not allow individuals to register in person for any reason.

31. Answer: b. $36.75
The exam fee to take the Florida Real Estate Licensing Exam for Sales Associates is $36.75.

32. Answer: b. 48 hours before your scheduled exam
You are allowed to reschedule or cancel your real estate licensing exam, without penalty, up until 48 hours before your scheduled exam.

33. Answer: d. Both A and B
You will forfeit your right to a full refund if you are absent on the day of your testing appointment or if you arrive late on testing day and miss the time of your testing appointment.

34. Answer: a. Supporting documents
If you miss your testing appointment, there are a few reasons that may be excused, such as serious illness, a death in the family or a family

emergency. In order to qualify for an excused absence, you will be required to provide supporting documents for the absence, such as a doctor's note or an obituary.

35. Answer: b. 30 minutes before your appointment
Pearson VUE asks that all individuals who are testing show up at least 30 minutes before their scheduled testing time to ensure they can check in on time for their exam and provide the testing facility with appropriate personal information and identification.

36. Answer: c. Left in the locker provided by the testing facility
Pearson VUE asks that you limit the personal items you bring with you and gives you a place to put any personal items.

37. Answer: d. Using a testing facility computer
The Florida Real Estate Licensing Exam is administered electronically on a computer provided by the testing facility.

38. Answer: b. 15 minutes
You will be given about 15 minutes to become familiar with the computer and how to navigate the program.

39. Answer: a. The computer and program
The test administrators are permitted to answer only questions regarding the computer program and test-taking instructions.

40. Answer: c. Three and a half hours
You will be given three and a half hours to complete your real estate licensing exam.

41. Answer: c. 100
The Florida Real Estate Licensing Exam has 100 multiple-choice questions.

42. Answer: d. 75/100
To pass the licensing exam, you are required to score a minimum of 75 out of 100.

43. Answer: a. A mortgage loan that has a fluctuating interest rate
A mortgage that has an interest rate that changes is an adjustable mortgage.

44. Answer: b. An appraisal
An individual who is educated, qualified and licensed in the State of Florida to conduct a review of a property and then place a valuation on that property based on those findings is a licensed appraiser, and the formal statement of their findings is called an appraisal.

45. Answer: c. A balloon payment
A balloon payment requires a large sum to be paid all at once. The amount of a balloon payment is significantly larger than the typical monthly payment for the loan. Sometimes this provision happens annually; sometimes it happens only once in the life of a loan. The terms vary from contract to contract.

46. Answer: a. $29,511.00
To find Sally's commission, multiply the sale price with the percentage of the commission.

47. Answer: b. $169,983.00
To find Davis' commission, add the sale price of the Tango Bar and Grill to the closing costs and multiply that by the percentage of the commission.

48. Answer: c. $58,010.61
Add the sale price of the beach house to half of its closing costs. Multiply the total by 7% to find the commission earned.

49. Answer: d. $796,980.90
Add the sale price of the ski lodge to the closing costs of the sale. Multiply the total by Kelly's 30% commission.

50. Answer: b. 3 square feet
Multiply the width of the flower bed in feet (0.5 ft.) by the length in feet (6 ft.) to give the area.

51. Answer: d. 97.2 %
To find the loan-to-value ratio on the townhouse, take the down payment and the mortgage amount, the sum of which is the sale price. Divide the mortgage by the sale price. 350,000 / 360,000. This will give you the loan-to-value ratio.

52. Answer: a. $36
To find the adjustable rental rate, divide the increased index by the original index: $3.0 \div 2.5 = 1.2$. Then multiply this proportion by the cost per square foot they are currently paying: $1.2 \times \$30 = \$36$.

53. Answer: b. $25.34

To find the adjustable rental rate of the warehouse, take the increased index divided by the original index. Multiply the answer by the current rent of $12.20 per square foot.

54. Answer: c. $30.41
To find the adjustable rental rate of the downtown club, divide the increased index by the original index: $4.7 \div 3.4 = 1.3824$. Multiply this proportion by the rent per square foot: $1.382 \times \$22 = \$30.41$.

55. Answer: d. $1,193.56
To define the adjustable rental rate of the midtown high-rise, divide the increased index of 72.94 by the original index of 46.75. Multiply the answer by the original rental price per square foot to give the adjustable rental rate.

56. Answer: b. Absentee owner
When a property owner acts as landlord for a property he/she owns but does not reside in or when a property owner hires a brokerage to manage a property where tenants, instead of the owner, live, the owner is known as an absentee owner.

57. Answer: c. A legal clause that binds the contracted party
In the event that the contract is broken, the lender may demand from the borrower immediate payment in full on any remaining balance. This is called an acceleration clause.

58. Answer: d. Ad valorem
Ad valorem is the legal term that refers to a property's value being used to calculate the taxes that are owed on the property.

59. Answer: a. Arbitration

Arbitration is the legal term that refers to parties bringing a legal matter before a judge alone rather than in front of a jury, presenting their sides and evidence to the judge, and the judge making a final ruling over the issues.

60. Answer: b. Blockbusting
Blockbusting is when a broker or sales associate uses fear and intimidation to pressure a seller into selling quickly, at a loss, so the sales associate can sell the property at a higher price for a much higher return.

61. Answer: c. Building codes
Local government uses these legal guidelines to ensure that new construction and remodels to existing properties are done in a standardized way.

62. Answer: d. Building permit
City or county government requires a building permit any time remodeling, demolition, construction, additions or other such building projects are taking place. Building permits allow a city to know the kind of renovations that are being done and to ensure that they are zoned properly.

63. Answer: a. A legal action in which a notice is placed in a newspaper, and possibly other public forums, to inform of legal action that is being taken when the individual or party the action is taken against cannot be reached personally

64. Answer: b. Contract
A contract is a legally binding document between individuals or parties that outlines the terms of their agreement, the stipulations that will be

applied should the agreement be broken by one or both parties, and any miscellaneous terms the parties have agreed on.

65. Answer: c. Culpable negligence
Culpable negligence is the legal term that describes when a sales associate, broker or other real estate representative neglects a customer or client to the point that it causes financial harm or damage to the other party.

66. Answer: d. Easement
An easement is a legal permission for an individual to use a portion of the property that belongs to someone else. This is generally used when one person's property is in front of another's and the only way to reach that property is through their neighbor. For example, James has a four-acre plot right on the main road; there are no other access roads that go to the property behind his for miles. Brandon bought four acres from James, directly behind James' property. In their purchase contract, James made a concession to Brandon for an easement through James' property so Brandon can reach his. The easement is Brandon's driveway, running along the left side of James' property.

67. Answer: a. Due-on-sale clause
A due-on-sale clause can be found in a mortgage contract. It requires the borrower to pay any remaining balance on the mortgage if he/she sells the property that the mortgage is on before the mortgage is brought to a zero balance.

68. Answer: b. Eminent domain
Eminent domain is a legal action that local, state or federal government can use. When a government agency uses the eminent domain provision, it compensates the property owner at a fair market value and takes that

property to be repurposed for public use. For example, a city is expanding Main Street to be five lanes instead of three. The city buys 12 feet of land from where the road currently is into the private property of the people who live along the main road. That land is then used to accommodate the widening of a public highway.

69. Answer: c. Encroachment
An individual is encroaching on property if they are trespassing on the property of a neighbor.

70. Answer: d. Escheat
Escheat is the legal right expressed by the state when a resident of that state dies with no will and no family. The state is then allowed to take ownership of that property since there is no one who is legally entitled to it and the owner is no longer alive.

71. Answer: a. Estate for years
The estate for years is a legally binding lease between two parties that has a start date and a set end date.

72. Answer: b. Exempt property
When a property is taxed but the property's value is not used to calculate that tax, that property is known as an exempt property.

73. Answer: c. Further assurance
Further assurance is when a legal document is provided during a sale or purchase. The document states that the property's title is "free and clear." This means that there are no liens or debts that can be levied against that property.

74. Answer: d. Handicap status
A handicap status is given to individuals who have physical or mental deficits that inhibit their activities to the point at which those deficits affect daily life, the ability to complete day-to-day tasks and the ability to care for themselves entirely independently.

75. Answer: a. Health ordinance
A health ordinance is usually overseen and dictated by the local government. Laws that fall under a health ordinance are all put in place for the health, safety and well-being of the community.

76. Answer: b. Homestead Law
The Homestead Law was put in place to protect surviving spouses, minor children and unmarried children from losing their homes when the head of the household dies. It protects the property against things such as debt collectors, creditors and lien holders to prevent the loss of a home when the homeowner or head of the household dies.

77. Answer: c. Interpleader
Interpleader is a term that describes when a legal judgment is made to determine who is legally entitled to funds or who those funds belong to when pertaining to real estate matters.

78. Answer: d. Lien
A lender or creditor can use a lien, which gives him/her a legal claim to personal property in the event that the borrower is in default. Most commonly, collateral is used to secure a loan or mortgage. A lien prevents the property owner from selling or liquidating any property that has a claim on it until the borrower has repaid the debt.

79. Answer: a. Liquidated damages

Liquidated damages are a sum charge to an individual, party or entity in breach of contract. This is often seen in rental properties, such as apartment complexes, when a tenant is on a lease for a specific number of months and leaves before that time period is up. For example, a property manager leases an apartment for $300 a month for the next 12 months. The property manager expects to earn $3,600 off that property for the year. If the tenant for whatever reason moves out early, breaking the lease, the property manager loses out on the rent he would have earned if the tenant had fulfilled the contract. Liquidated damages are generally charged so that the tenant who broke the lease pays for at least a portion of the amount of money the property manager lost from the person moving out early.

80. Answer: b. Lis pendens

Lis pendens is a legal term that means a party or parties are being informed that legal action is being taken.

81. Answer: c. Placing a 30-year limit on title matter defects

The Marketable Record Title Act of Chapter 712 of the Florida Statutes places a limit of 30 years on certain matters in regard to title matter defects. If a chain of title is maintained on a property and that title is 30 years old or older, certain liens and levies can no longer be held against that property.

82. Answer: d. Mediation

When there is a legal dispute, rather than taking the argument directly to a court of law, the parties may agree to mediation. This means that all parties involved will sit down with a non-biased third party who has no legal, personal or financial stake in the disagreement. The mediator will attempt to help the disputing parties involved come to an agreement on the matter without having to take it before a judge.

83. Answer: a. Nolo contendere

Nolo contendere is a Latin term used within the legal system that simply means "no contest." To not contest a legal matter means that a complaint was raised and the party involved is not disputing the claim, but he/she is not saying that he/she is guilty of the matter for which the complaint was filed. For example, Peter gets a speeding ticket. He goes to court and pays the fine for the ticket but does not enter a plea of guilty for his traffic infraction. By paying the fine, he is choosing not to contest his charge for speeding.

84. Answer: b. Nonconforming use

Nonconforming use is the ability to legally continue the preexisting use of a property for a purpose the area it resides in is no longer zoned for.

85. Answer: c. Note

In the world of real estate, lending a note refers to a legal document that shows a debt owed.

86. Answer: d. A set of laws made for the health, safety and welfare of the public

Police powers are a legal right, but the local government can act on when they exercise powers that are used for the common health and welfare of the general public and community.

87. Answer: a. Probable cause

Probable cause is a legal term that means one party has a justifiable reason or evidence to support seeking legal or disciplinary actions.

88. Answer: b. Redlining

In real estate and lending, when an individual, party or business refuses to lend funds for purchases because of the specific area or demographic of the borrower, this is known as redlining. Redlining is discriminatory, and in the world of real estate it goes against several laws, including the Fair Housing Act.

89. Answer: c. Special exception

When a property is used in a way that it is not zoned for or in an area in which it goes against use laws, an exception that is made for that property to conduct business is known as a special exception.

90. Answer: d. Statute of frauds

Statute of frauds is the legal requirement for certain agreements and contracts to be put in writing in order for them to be legally binding. Those issues that fall under the statute of frauds are enforceable only if they are in writing. If there is a legal dispute on a subject that falls under this term and it is not in writing, there is nothing the courts can legally do to remedy the situation.

91. Answer: a. Statute of limitations

A statute of limitations means that an individual, group or entity can seek legal action on a matter as long as it is done in a specific time frame. For example, murder generally has no statute of limitations, so if it takes 50 years to find the criminal who committed the act, he/she can be charged for the crimes when found. On the other hand, there may be a window of only eight years during which a victim of domestic violence can seek legal action to punish the person who caused harm. If the injured party does not take legal action in those eight years, once that time is over, the injured party cannot seek retribution.

92. Answer: b. Subpoena

A subpoena is a legal document issued by the courts and delivered to an individual or multiple individuals requiring the person or persons to appear before a court of law at the date and time listed in the documents. Failure to heed a subpoena can result in fines and jail time.

93. Answer: c. Unenforceable

Legally unenforceable is a term that means you cannot seek out legal action, and legal action cannot be thrust on an individual over an unenforceable action.

94. Answer: d. Valid

A contract is valid when the terms of that contract are met and enforceable. If you were to break the terms of a contract, it could make the agreement invalid and no longer guarantee you the provisions that were made in the agreement prior to the breach.

95. Answer: a. It is not legally enforceable

If a contract is null or void, it is not legally enforceable.

96. Answer: b. The Florida Real Estate Commission

Title 32, Chapter 475.02 of the Florida statutes outlines the responsibilities of the Florida Real Estate Commission.

97. Answer: c. The Division of Real Estate

Title 32, Chapter 475.021 outlines the services provided by the Division of Real Estate.

98. Answer: d. Both A and B.
Under Florida law, the Florida Real Estate Commission Education and Research Foundation are required to be involved in educational expansion and evolving continued education programs for sales associates and brokers.

99. Answer: a. The Florida Real Estate Commission
The Florida Real Estate Commission is responsible for much of the criteria, training and disciplinary actions for real estate associates.

100. Answer: b. Fees
Under Title 32, Chapter 475.125 of the Florida statutes, the Florida Real Estate Commission and the Florida Department of Business and Professional Regulation are responsible for the fees associated with the education, examination, licensing and continued education of sales associates.

# Sales Associates Practice Test 2

1. Under Title 39, Chapter 680 of the Florida statutes, the Florida Statute of Fraud law was put in place for which of the following reasons?
   a. To prevent all parties involved in an agreement from committing fraud in regard to the sale or purchase of real property
   b. To prevent individuals from providing false financial information in order to qualify for mortgage financing
   c. To outline the terms between any two parties regarding any legal matter
   d. To protect the buyer in the event that the seller fails to disclose information that was pertinent in the purchase of the property

2. Under what Florida law are lenders required to file a lawsuit in state court against a borrower to render judgment on the borrower's default on a loan?
   a. Fair Housing Act
   b. Florida foreclosure law
   c. Florida Homestead Act
   d. Green Belt Law

3. Under Florida foreclosure law, a borrower is given ___ to respond to the state court after being served for a complaint lodged by a lender.
   a. 7 days
   b. 14 days
   c. 20 days
   d. 30 days

4. Under Florida foreclosure law, if a borrower does not respond by the deadline set by the courts, a/an ____ will be granted to the lender.
    a. Summary judgment
    b. Conviction
    c. Default judgment
    d. Exoneration

5. If a borrower can provide an adequate excuse or counterclaim against the lender for justification of nonpayment, then a judge:
    a. May dismiss the matter entirely
    b. May move for summary judgment
    c. May make a default judgment on the matter
    d. May deny the lender's motion and proceed to discovery

6. Under Florida foreclosure law, the foreclosure process may be expedited if the borrower:
    a. Does not contest the foreclosure
    b. Contests the foreclosure
    c. Provides adequate proof to support his/her nonpayment
    d. Refuses to leave the home without force

7. When a lender is ruled in favor of foreclosure by Florida State courts, the property will be placed for sale no sooner than ____ days from the time the judgment is made and no more than ____ days from that same judgment.
    a. 7 days, 14 days
    b. 20 days, 35 days
    c. 30 days, 60 days
    d. 30 days, 90 days

8. Under Florida law, a notice of foreclosure must be published publicly for two consecutive weeks, and there must be two publications placed, at least five days apart, before the property goes up for auction in a foreclosure sale. Where is the notification required to appear?
   a. Online
   b. On a billboard
   c. In a newspaper
   d. On a for-sale sign

9. In the event that a property is sold and the former occupant does not move out of the property before the new property owner takes possession, which of the following, permitted under Florida law, can be used to have the former owner leave the home or property?
   a. Cash-for-keys deal
   b. Forced removal
   c. Eviction
   d. Trespassing complaint

10. Following a foreclosure auction, a certificate of sale must be filed with the county clerk's office by:
   a. The time that the auction is concluded
   b. The next business day after the sale took place
   c. The end of the week in which the sale took place
   d. The end of the month in which the sale took place

11. The legal process for selling a property that is being foreclosed on in which the property is sold to the highest bidder is known as a/an:
   a. Appraisal
   b. Acquisition
   c. Auction
   d. Annuity

12. In what year was the Florida Community Planning Act enacted?
    a. 1991
    b. 2001
    c. 2005
    d. 2011

13. The Florida law that puts local government in control of community development is called:
    a. The Historic Preservation Act
    b. The Marketable Record Title Act
    c. The Florida Homestead Act
    d. The Community Planning Act

14. Which entity, under the Community Planning Act, is responsible for the organizing and running of community planning?
    a. The Florida Real Estate Commission
    b. The Division of Real Estate
    c. The Division of Community Planning
    d. The Department of Community Affairs

15. Under the Community Planning Act, all of the following are the responsibility of the Division of Community Development except for:
    a. Community zoning
    b. The sale of city property
    c. Land-use restrictions
    d. Building codes

16. The Division of Community Development has five specific labels for land use. These labels include residential, commercial, industrial, agricultural and special use. These labels are legally known as:
    a. Zoning
    b. Building permits
    c. Building codes
    d. Land use restrictions

17. The legal term for laws, rules and guidelines that protect community safety and health is:
    a. Zoning ordinance
    b. Building codes
    c. Certificate of occupancy
    d. Building permit

18. The Community Planning Act requires, through local government, that each building be inspected before it is allowed to be opened and occupied. This is known as:
    a. Appraisal
    b. Comparative market analysis
    c. Building inspection
    d. Open house

19. Under the Florida Marketable Record Title Act there are two types of title insurance. These are:
    a. Borrower policy and mortgage policy
    b. Mortgagor policy and lender policy
    c. Tenant policy and landlord policy
    d. Owner policy and lender policy

20. The Florida Marketable Record Title Act was first enacted in which of the following years?
    a. 1923
    b. 1963
    c. 1993
    d. 2003

21. The Florida Marketable Record Title Act puts a limit of ____ during which title defects can apply to specific titles. After that point, the title defects are void and fall off the title.
    a. 10 years
    b. 20 years
    c. 30 years
    d. 40 years

22. The Florida Marketable Record Title Act provides which of the following provisions to a title after 30 years?
    a. A chain of title
    b. A new title
    c. New restrictions
    d. Invalidates and cures defects

23. In what year was the Civil Rights Act established as federal law?
    a. 1866
    b. 1966
    c. 1996
    d. 2006

24. After which of the following events was the Civil Rights Act made into law?
    a. The Cold War
    b. The Civil War
    c. The Great Depression
    d. The Vietnam War

25. The Civil Rights Act was enacted to abolish discrimination based on which of the following reasons?
    a. Gender
    b. Religion
    c. Race
    d. Citizenship

26. In what year was the Civil Rights Act expanded to include color, religion, sex and national origin?
    a. 1994
    b. 1984
    c. 1974
    d. 1964

27. In 1968, the Civil Rights Act was absorbed into which of the following acts to include discrimination in the housing market?
    a. The Fair Housing Act
    b. The Americans with Disabilities Act
    c. The Superfund Amendments and Reauthorization Act
    d. The Home Mortgage Disclosure Act

28. The Fair Housing Act includes single-family homes and multifamily homes in residential properties when doing which of the following?
   a. Selling
   b. Purchasing
   c. Renting
   d. All of the above

29. In which of the following years was the Fair Housing Act amended to include disabled individuals and families with disabled children?
   a. 2008
   b. 1998
   c. 1988
   d. 1898

30. Pertaining to the Fair Housing Act, handicapped individuals are defined as those with ____ and/or ____ impairments that limit or seriously hinder their everyday activities.
   a. Social and/or emotional
   b. Auditory and/or verbal
   c. Sensory and/or motor function
   d. Physical and/or mental

31. The Fair Housing Act was later expanded to include provisions for:
   a. Pregnant women
   b. Veterans
   c. Elderly individuals
   d. Migrant workers

32. Which of the following does the Fair Housing Act make exceptions for in regard to selling or leasing?
    a. Retirement communities
    b. Condominiums
    c. Timeshares
    d. Apartment complexes

33. The Fair Housing Act makes exceptions in regard to retirement communities, which require their residents to be ____ or older.
    a. 55 years of age
    b. 60 years of age
    c. 62 years of age
    d. 74 years of age

34. Developments that have a minimum of ____ of their units or homes occupied by individuals who are 55 years of age or older are also given an exception under the Fair Housing Act, so long as that development also provides senior-citizen-oriented activities or amenities.
    a. 50%
    b. 60%
    c. 70%
    d. 80%

35. Generally, the Fair Housing Act does not apply to which of the following situations?
    a. "For Sale by Owner" properties
    b. Executive apartments
    c. Extended stay accommodations
    d. Townhouse purchases

36. Under which federal law are property owners and real estate brokers not permitted to refuse showings, sales, purchases, leases or negotiations?
    a. Eminent domain law
    b. Fair Housing Act
    c. Americans with Disabilities Act
    d. Interstate Land Sales Full Disclosure Act

37. In what year was the Americans with Disabilities Act enacted?
    a. 1909
    b. 1980
    c. 1990
    d. 2009

38. The Americans with Disabilities Act protects which of the following classes of individuals?
    a. Female individuals
    b. Disabled individuals
    c. Homeless individuals
    d. Terminal individuals

39. In addition to preventing discrimination toward disabled or handicapped individuals, the Americans with Disabilities Act also requires which of the following to be met?
    a. Exclusive services that can be received only by handicapped individuals
    b. Designated areas for individuals with disabilities only
    c. Access and accommodation to public facilities and transportation
    d. Free entry to public accommodation for disabled individuals

40. As of ____, all new construction must meet the Americans with Disabilities Act specifications, including things like wheelchair ramps and wider doorways.

   a. 1980
   b. 1990
   c. 2000
   d. 2010

41. The Interstate Land Sales Full Disclosure Act pertains to bulk property purchases of more than ___ lots.

   a. 5
   b. 25
   c. 75
   d. 150

42. Under the Interstate Land Sales Full Disclosure Act, individuals are permitted a window of ____ in which they can suspend an offer if a property report is not provided to them in a timely manner.

   a. 7 days
   b. 14 days
   c. 24 days
   d. 36 days

43. When negotiating the purchase of bulk property under the Interstate Land Sales Full Disclosure Act, buyers are permitted to receive a full refund of any deposits if they suspend any contract within which of the following time frames?

   a. 12 months
   b. 24 months
   c. 36 months
   d. 72 months

44. Which of the following pieces of legislature did the United States government enact in 1980 in order to clean up and make financial amends for hazardous substances that pose a risk to the safety and well-being of the public?
    a. Clean Water and Air Act
    b. Florida Community Planning Act
    c. Comprehensive Environmental Response, Compensation and Liability Act
    d. Interstate Land Sales Full Disclosure Act

45. For which of the following reasons was the National Priorities List created?
    a. To list United States priorities from most to least important
    b. To identify endangered species on American soil
    c. To organize areas of high risk in order from highest priority to least
    d. To identify contaminated property sites

46. Anna has an estimated monthly housing expense of $945, and her monthly obligations total $1,682. If Anna has a monthly gross income of $3,620, what is the total obligations ratio?
    a. 45%
    b. 46%
    c. 47%
    d. 50%

47. Blake has an estimated monthly business expense of $2,250, and his monthly obligations total $3,600. If Blake has a monthly gross income of $7,654, what is the total obligations ratio?
    a. 27%
    b. 37%
    c. 47%
    d. 57%

48. Evelyn applies for a 30-year mortgage of $145,000 at 5.25% interest. How much of the $4,200 monthly payment, paid in the second month, will apply to the principal?

   a. $634.38
   b. $618.78
   c. $35,654.62
   d. $3,581.22

49. Aaron moves from Dallas to Pittsburgh. He signs a lease moving into his apartment on June 12. The rent for the apartment is $875 a month. The landlord will prorate the rent for the month of June, and Aaron will pay only for the days he is actually living in the apartment, so he is charged a prorated rent only from June 12 to June 30 and the move-in date is not included in the calculation. What is Aaron's prorated rent for June?

   a. $525.00
   b. $345.00
   c. $29.17
   d. $634.38

50. Hailey rents a beach house for seven days at the end of July. The beach house rents for $1,600 a month. The landlord prorates the rent and charges Hailey only for the days she will be renting the beach house, plus a daily upcharge of 3% of the daily rent. What will the prorated rent for the week be?

   a. $51.61
   b. $53.16
   c. $372.13
   d. $525.00

51. Beth is appraising a one-year-old townhome. The total livable square footage is 4,250. The two-car garage is 800 square feet. The estimated cost per square foot is $62 for the livable area and $31 for the garage. What is the reproduction cost new (RCN) for the property?
    a. $263,500
    b. $24,800
    c. $288,300
    d. $576,600

52. Felix sells his hardware store for $984,650; the closing costs are $9,846.00. His broker, Dolly, gets a commission of 8% of the sale. How much is Dolly's commission?
    a. $78,772
    b. $87,200
    c. $79,559.68
    d. $79,000

53. Gators Putt-Putt Golf sells for $2,500,000; closing costs are $25,000. Kale, the broker who sold the property, gets a 32% commission. How much is Kale's commission?
    a. $8,800
    b. $88,000
    c. $808,000
    d. $880,000

54. Bella sells her craft shop for $987,600; the closing costs are $98,760. The buyer is paying half of the closing costs. Her broker, Barry, is earning a 12% commission. How much is Barry's commission?
    a. $119.03
    b. $100,019.00
    c. $120,000.00
    d. $124,437.60

55. Anna sells her French chateau for $26,000,000; the closing costs are $200,000. Anna's broker, Audrea, is earning a 32% commission from the sale. How much is Audrea's commission for this sale?
    a. $8,384,000
    b. $83,840
    c. $183,640
    d. $762,945

56. The Willow Subdivision is located two blocks from the business district in Valley Springs. The parcel of land that separates the subdivision from the business district property is known as a:
    a. Vacant lot
    b. Development
    c. Farm area
    d. Buffer zone

57. To keep the public and community safe, the local government has strict:
    a. Building codes
    b. Zoning
    c. Building permits
    d. Citations

58. A building inspector must issue a/an ____ in order for a new building to open to the public or be lived in by owners or tenants.
    a. Building permit
    b. Certificate of occupancy
    c. Appraisal
    d. Citation

59. A sales associate or broker reviews properties that have recently sold that are located in the same general area and have similarities to a property that he/she is planning to list. Then the sales associate or broker uses the information gathered to help the property owners decide on a fair list price that is appropriate for the current market. This is known as:

   a. Cost-depreciation approach
   b. Consent to transition
   c. Comparative market analysis
   d. Discount point

60. Tom owns several acres behind Bill's property. The only road in the area is in front of Bill's property, and there are no other access roads for Tom to reach his property. When Bill sold the acreage behind his home, the men added provisions for a/an ____ to the contract so that Tom would always have legal access to his property.

   a. Deed restriction
   b. Eminent domain
   c. Exempt property
   d. Easement

61. Anna is a sales associate at Neman Brokerage. Bethany arranges for Anna to help her look for a buyer for the real estate Bethany wants to sell. Anna and Bethany sign a contract or agreement that allows Anna to get a commission *only* if she is the one to find a buyer. Bethany can still look for a buyer, and if she finds one, she will not pay Anna a commission. The condition on that agreement is that Bethany does not list her property with any other agents or brokerages. This is known as:

   a. Exclusive agency listing
   b. Exclusive right of sell
   c. Exculpatory clause
   d. Equity of redemption

62. Loans that are either funded, insured or protected by the United States government are:
    a. Federal Housing Administration loans
    b. Federally related transactions
    c. Fair Housing Act loans
    d. Freehold estates

63. When the United States government uses surveyors to mark any area of government property, this is called a:
    a. General warranty deed
    b. Legal description
    c. Government survey system
    d. Like-kind exchange

64. Skyler got a new job offer and decided to move from Michigan to Washington, D.C., right away. To do so, she had to break the lease on the townhouse she was renting in Michigan. The landlord bills her for a set amount as a result of terminating her contract early. This charge is known as a:
    a. Security deposit
    b. Gross lease
    c. Percentage lease
    d. Liquidated damages

65. Zachary and his wife bought an older home five years ago. Over the last five years, the couple has invested substantially in remodeling and improving the property. After having the property appraised, their realtor informed them that they would not see a return on much of the money they had invested because a majority of improvements looked nice but actually added no value to the home. This is known as:
    a. Over-improvement
    b. Nonconforming use
    c. Redlining
    d. Special assessment

66. Terra owns a home on the Florida Gulf Coast. The house is a beautiful beachfront property. It is late spring and Terra's home is one of the only properties for sale in her area. Her realtor informs her that he has shown her home to several prospective buyers and has several offers, especially because her home is the only one in the area for sale. This is known as:
    a. Buyer's market
    b. Open listing
    c. Seller's market
    d. Regression

67. Avery and Emily pay $2,500 a year to spend July 1 through July 10 at a beach house in Hawaii. During that time every year, they are guaranteed that the house is theirs alone. This arrangement is known as a:
    a. Lease
    b. Rental
    c. Sublease
    d. Timeshare

68. Kate owns a craft shop at the intersection of Lennox and Main. The description for a property that is located at an intersection like this is called a/an:

   a. Easement
   b. Parcel
   c. Corner lot
   d. Plot

69. Aaron has owned a bookstore on the poor side of town for 15 years. A real estate developer then came in and vastly improved the area, breathing new life into it. Because of the developer's improvements, Aaron's bookstore has increased in value. What is this known as?

   a. Redlining
   b. Key lot
   c. Progression
   d. Novation

70. Kenny is the manager of an apartment complex downtown. Halfway through the month, Marion applies to rent an apartment and is approved. She will be moving in mid-month, and Kenny will be charging her for only the days she will be actually living in the apartment that month. This practice is known as:

   a. Vacancy rate
   b. Reconciliation
   c. Payment clause
   d. Proration

71. As a real estate sales associate, you will be supervised by:
    a. An office manager
    b. A leasing consultant
    c. A broker
    d. A senior sales associate

72. A broker will be ____ for your actions while you are performing real estate duties.
    a. Watching
    b. Liable
    c. Coercing
    d. Counseling

73. The home you are assigned to list has asbestos countertops in the kitchen. A specialized team is hired to remove the countertops since the product is considered a/an:
    a. Incredibly heavy material
    b. Property fixture
    c. Permanent landmark
    d. Environmental hazard

74. Torrie sold a newlywed couple a new home two weeks ago. Today she calls the couple to touch base. This practice is called:
    a. Follow-up
    b. Solicitation
    c. Further assurance
    d. Benchmark

75. If a sales associate is given any money for real estate transactions, it is his/her responsibility to turn that money over to the broker within:
  a. 12 hours
  b. 24 hours
  c. 48 hours
  d. 72 hours

76. Sales associates often conduct:
  a. Closings
  b. Appraisals
  c. Open houses
  d. Audits

77. An important job as a sales associate is to build and facilitate ___ in your community or sales area.
  a. Developments
  b. Tenures
  c. Blockbusting
  d. Relationships

78. Florida has property in the Everglades, with waterfront properties around almost its entire coastline. With such abundance of waterways and ocean, it is no wonder that Florida has laws protecting and regulating:
  a. Waterfront properties
  b. Pools and spas
  c. Environmental hazards
  d. Exotic plant life

79. Sales associates are required to complete ___ hours of post-licensing education within the first 12 months after receiving their license. The post-education courses are required to be completed before the license is up for renewal.

   a. 14
   b. 16
   c. 45
   d. 72

80. After the first year, sales associates are required to complete ___ hours of continued education annually before the expiration date of their license. License renewal is contingent on this being completed.

   a. 12
   b. 14
   c. 16
   d. 18

81. Continued education allows sales associates to stay current on:

   a. Licensing penalties, fees and disciplinary actions
   b. Codes, zoning and laws
   c. Changes in licensing and continuing education requirements
   d. Both B and C

82. If you are working under a broker and the broker dies, your license will become ____ until you are hired under a new broker and the proper paperwork has been submitted.

   a. Involuntary inactive
   b. Void
   c. Suspended
   d. Expired

83. Another term for personal property is:

a. Intangible
b. Real estate
c. Chattel
d. Tangible

84. Specialized loans for service members are known as:

a. FHA loans
b. HUD
c. FHLMC loans
d. VA loans

85. To transition from being a sales associate to a broker, you must have actively worked in the field for __ years before you meet the required experience to take your broker's licensing exam.

a. 2
b. 3
c. 4
d. 5

86. To be eligible to become a real estate agent, you *must* have a/an:

a. High school diploma or GED
b. Associate's degree with a focus on real estate
c. Bachelor's degree with a major in real estate
d. The only requirement is your age

87. You will need an ___ Number when you schedule your appointment for digital fingerprinting.
    a. Original Realtor Induction
    b. Originating Agency Identification
    c. Originating Real Estate Intentions
    d. Ongoing Registration Identification

88. You can find a current list of approved Live Scan providers on the ___ website.
    a. Florida Real Estate Commission's
    b. Florida Department of Business and Professional Regulation's
    c. Florida Department of Law Enforcement's
    d. Florida Realtor Association's

89. If you have a criminal history, the Florida Real Estate Commission and/or the Department of Business and Professional Regulation will:
    a. Review your application and criminal history to determine if you are still eligible to become a real estate agent
    b. Reject your application immediately for failing to pass the background check and flag you as not being cleared to work in real estate
    c. Suspend your application and bar you from further activities in any professional careers in Florida
    d. Both B and C

90. Pearson VUE has 21 testing sites that offer testing ___ through ___.
    a. Monday, Saturday
    b. Sunday, Thursday
    c. Tuesday, Saturday
    d. Monday, Friday

91. Pearson VUE will accept reservations to take the Florida Real Estate Licensing Exam up until:
    a. The day of testing
    b. The day before testing
    c. Three days before testing
    d. Seven days before testing

92. If you are late for your exam, Pearson VUE will:
    a. Fit you in only if you pay extra charges
    b. Fit you in if they can
    c. Reschedule your exam for another day
    d. Bar you from registering again for 30 days

93. The testing center will operate year-round on a regular schedule of Monday through Saturday except for:
    a. Weekends
    b. Weekdays
    c. Tuesdays and Thursdays
    d. Major holidays

94. If you cannot pay your exam fee at the time you register, you may:
    a. Make arrangements to pay it before the exam date
    b. Make arrangements to pay it at the time of your exam
    c. Not register until you can pay the exam fee
    d. Apply and have the fee waived since you could not pay it

95. Pearson VUE allows those with disabilities to apply for accommodations to take the exam. These accommodations include all of the following except:
    a. Separate testing rooms
    b. A person or computer to fill the exam out
    c. Extra testing time
    d. A person or computer to read the exam

96. In order to be approved for testing accommodations, you will be required to:
    a. Provide supporting documents
    b. Be blind
    c. Use a wheelchair
    d. Have a note from a parent

97. Accommodations for testing will be provided:
    a. To everyone
    b. As needed
    c. When space is available
    d. For a fee

98. The dress code for exam day is:
    a. Casual
    b. Business casual
    c. Business professional
    d. Formal

99. You are required to bring ____ forms of ID when checking in for your state exam.

   a. 1
   b. 2
   c. 3
   d. 4

100. A real estate sales associate license must be renewed:

   a. Every year
   b. Every two years
   c. Every four years
   d. Every six years

# Answers – Sales Associates Practice Test 2

1. Answer: a. To prevent all parties involved in an agreement from committing fraud in regard to the sale or purchase of real property Title 39, Chapter 680 outlines this Florida statute.

2. Answer: b. Florida foreclosure law
   Under Florida foreclosure law, all lenders are required to file a lawsuit with the state court against a borrower in the event that the borrower defaults on a loan or mortgage in order for a judgment to be rendered and foreclosure proceedings to start taking place. The courts will notify the property owner of the lender's intentions, and the borrower will be given a set amount of time to respond to the courts regarding the matter.

3. Answer: c. 20 days
   Under Florida foreclosure law, a borrower must be given 20 days to respond to the courts after being served a complaint. The complaint is first made with the state court by the lender. The courts then notify the property owner that the lender has filed against him/her. From the day that the property owner is served notice, he/she has 20 days to reply to the courts.

4. Answer: c. Default judgment
   Under Florida foreclosure law, if a borrower does not respond to the state court by the deadline, the judge is then within his/her legal rights to make a default judgment, which will rule in favor of the lender's complaint because the borrower failed to respond. The lender is automatically allowed to proceed with foreclosure proceedings if this happens.

5. Answer: d. May deny the lender's motion and proceed to discovery
Protection is granted to a borrower under Florida foreclosure law if the borrower can provide an adequate excuse for nonpayment or a justifiable counterclaim against the lender. Florida foreclosure law allows the state court to delay foreclosure proceedings and move on to discovery proceedings. This will allow the courts and the parties involved to gather evidence and present it as to why their claims or counterclaims are valid.

6. Answer: a. Does not contest the foreclosure
After a lender starts foreclosure proceedings and files a suit with the state courts, the borrower is notified of the action. If the borrower chooses not to contest the foreclosure, under Florida foreclosure law proceedings can be expedited.

7. Answer: b. 20 days, 35 days
When the state courts rule in favor of a lender regarding foreclosure proceedings, the property will be placed for sale no sooner than 20 days from the time the judgment is made and no more than 35 days from that same judgment. The lender is required to place two notices in the newspaper; the second must come five days after the first, and they both must be done during the time leading up to the foreclosure auction.

8. Answer: c. In a newspaper
Under Florida law, a notice of foreclosure must be published publicly for two consecutive weeks, and there must be two publications, made at least five days apart from one another, in the 20 days before the property is allowed to go up for auction. This publication must be in the newspaper, but it can also be put up in other social forums as long as they are in addition to the newspaper posting.

9. Answer: a. Cash-for-keys deal
   In the event that a property is sold and the former occupant does not move out, some new property owners will offer a "cash-for-keys" deal to the previous owner if he/she will leave the home or property immediately or by a set deadline.

10. Answer: b. The next business day after the sale took place
    Following a foreclosure auction, a certificate of sale must be filed with the county clerk's office. This *must* be done no later than the next business day following the sale.

11. Answer: c. Auction
    An auction is a public event following a state court ruling in favor of a lender in a foreclosure complaint. The lender will place a public notice in the newspaper leading up to the sale. Anyone interested in buying the property will show up at the date and time listed for the auction. Prospective buyers will then bid on the home in a live auction and the highest bidder will be awarded the purchase.

12. Answer: d. 2011
    In 2011, the Florida Community Planning Act was enacted. This put community building and planning in the hands of the local government under the Division of Community Planning.

13. Answer: d. The Community Planning Act
    The Community Planning Act is a Florida law that was put in place for the control of community development.

14. Answer: c. The Division of Community Planning
The Division of Community Planning is responsible for organizing, overseeing and running community planning under the Community Development Act. This can include subdivision and strip-mall developments and community parks.

15. Answer: b. The sale of city property
Under the Community Planning Act, the sale of city property is not the responsibility of the Division of Community Development.

16. Answer: a. Zoning
The Division of Community Development has five specific labels or "zones" for land use. These zones include residential properties, commercial properties, industrial properties, agricultural properties and special-use properties.

17. Answer: b. Building codes
Building codes are laws, rules and guidelines that protect community safety and health. They require things such as building materials being a specific grade and quality (or higher) in order to be used in building structures and ensure that safety measures, like smoke detectors and sprinkler systems, are installed, just to name a few examples.

18. Answer: c. Building inspection
The Community Planning Act requires, through local government, that each building be inspected before it is allowed to be opened and occupied. When new builds or renovations are done, building inspectors will often visit several times during different stages to ensure the build is correct and up to code.

19. Answer: d. Owner policy and lender policy
    Under the Florida Marketable Record Title Act, there are two types of title insurance: owner policy and lender policy.

20. Answer: b. 1963
    The Florida Marketable Record Title Act was first enacted in 1963.

21. Answer: c. 30 years
    The Florida Marketable Record Title Act puts a limit of 30 years on title defects. This means that once you reach the 30-year mark, any defects or liens against the property will fall off and the title will be clean.

22. Answer: d. Invalidates and cures defects
    The Florida Marketable Record Title Act overrides and cures defects on titles after 30 years. This does not apply to every case—there are some exceptions—but as a whole, it frees up most titles.

23. Answer: a. 1866
    The Civil Rights Act was established as a federal law in 1866.

24. Answer: b. The Civil War
    After the Civil War, the Civil Rights Act was made into law.

25. Answer: c. Race
    The Civil Rights Act was enacted to abolish discrimination based on race.

26. Answer: d. 1964
The Civil Rights Act was expanded to include color, religion, sex and national origin in 1964.

27. Answer: a. The Fair Housing Act
The Civil Rights Act was absorbed into the Fair Housing Act to include discrimination in the housing market.

28. Answer: d. All of the above
The Fair Housing Act includes single-family homes and multifamily homes in residential properties when selling, purchasing and renting.

29. Answer: c. 1988
The Fair Housing Act of 1988 includes disabled individuals and families with disabled children.

30. Answer: d. Physical and/or mental
Pertaining to the Fair Housing Act, handicapped individuals are defined as those with physical and/or mental impairments that limit or seriously hinder everyday activities.

31. Answer: a. Pregnant women
The Fair Housing Act was expanded to include provisions for pregnant women.

32. Answer: a. Retirement communities
The Fair Housing Act makes exceptions in regard to selling or leasing in retirement communities.

33. Answer: c. 62 years of age
The Fair Housing Act makes exceptions in regard to retirement communities that require their residents to be 62 years of age or older.

34. Answer: d. 80%
Eighty percent of units or homes must be occupied by individuals who are 55 years of age or older in order for a senior citizen development to be given an exception under the Fair Housing Act.

35. Answer: a. "For Sale by Owner" properties
Generally, the Fair Housing Act does not apply to "For Sale by Owner" properties.

36. Answer: b. Fair Housing Act
Under the Fair Housing Act, property owners and real estate brokers are not permitted to refuse showings, sales, purchases, leases or negotiations.

37. Answer: c. 1990
The Americans with Disabilities Act was enacted in 1990.

38. Answer: b. Disabled individuals
The Americans with Disabilities Act protects disabled individuals. It also covers pregnant women and families with disabled children.

39. Answer: c. Access and accommodations to public facilities and transportation
In addition to preventing discrimination toward disabled or handicapped individuals, the Americans with Disabilities Act also requires access and accommodation to public facilities and transportation.

40. Answer: b. 1990

Since 1990, all new construction must meet the Americans with Disabilities Act code specifications. Additionally, any renovations and remodeling must also meet such standards.

41. Answer: b. 25

The Interstate Land Sales Full Disclosure Act pertains to bulk property purchases of more than 25 lots.

42. Answer: a. 7 days

Under the Interstate Land Sales Full Disclosure Act, buyers are permitted to have a window of seven days in which they can rescind or pull out of an offer. They may do so if a property report is not provided to them in a timely manner.

43. Answer: b. 24 months

When negotiating the purchase of bulk property under the Interstate Land Sales Full Disclosure Act, buyers are permitted a full refund of any deposits if they rescind any bulk property purchase or sale contracts within 24 months of beginning the contract negotiation process.

44. Answer: c. Comprehensive Environmental Response, Compensation and Liability Act

The United States government enacted the Comprehensive Environmental Response, Compensation and Liability Act in 1980 in order to clean up and make financial amends for hazardous substances that pose a risk to the safety and well-being of the public.

45. Answer: d. To identify contaminated property sites
To identify contaminated properties, the National Priorities List was created.

46. Answer: b. 46%
Anna's total obligations ratio is 46%.

47. Answer: c. 47%
Blake's total obligations ratio is 47%.

48. Answer: d. $3,581.22
$3,581.22 will be applied to the principal in the second month.

49. Answer: a. $525.00
The prorated rent for Aaron's apartment is $525.00.

50. Answer: c. $372.13
The prorated rent for Hailey's beach house is $372.13.

51. Answer: c. $288,300
The reproduction cost new on Beth's townhome is $288,300.

52. Answer: c. $79,559.68
Dolly's commission is $79,559.68.

53. Answer: c. $808,000
Kale's commission is $808,000.

54. Answer: d. $124,437.60
Barry's commission is $124,437.60.
98,760/ 2 = 49,380
49,380 + 987,600 = 1,036,980
1,036,980 x 12 / 100 = $124,437.60

55. Answer: a. $8,384,000
Audrea's commission is $8,384,000.

56. Answer: d. Buffer zone
The Willow Subdivision is located two blocks from the business district in Valley Springs. The parcel of land that separates the subdivision from the business district property is known as the buffer zone.

57. Answer: a. Building codes
To keep the public and community safe, the local government has strict building codes.

58. Answer: b. Certificate of occupancy
A building inspector must issue a certificate of occupancy in order for a new building to open or be lived in.

59. Answer: c. Comparative market analysis
When a sales associate or broker reviews properties that have recently sold in the same general area and with similarities to a property that he/she is planning to list, and then uses the information gathered to help the property owners decide on a fair list price for the current market, this is known as a comparative market analysis.

60. Answer: d. Easement
An easement will allow Tom to have legal access to his property even if it is on Bill's land.

61. Answer: a. Exclusive agency listing
If Bethany does not list her property with any other agents or brokerages, this is known as an exclusive agency listing.

62. Answer: b. Federally related transactions
Loans that are either funded, insured or protected by the United States government are federally related transactions.

63. Answer: c. Government survey system
When the United States government uses surveyors to mark any area of government property, this is called a government survey system.

64. Answer: d. Liquidated damages
This charge is known as liquidated damages.

65. Answer: a. Over-improvement
When a realtor states someone will not see a return on much of the money invested because improvements on a property look nice but add no value to the home, this is known as over-improvement.

66. Answer: c. Seller's market
When a market favors people looking for properties instead of those selling them, this is known as a buyers' market.

67. Answer: d. Timeshare
This arrangement is known as a timeshare.

68. Answer: c. Corner lot
A property that is located at an intersection is called a corner lot.

69. Answer: b. Key lot
Aaron's property is known as a key lot.

70. Answer: d. Proration
Charging for only the days a person will be actually living in an apartment is known as proration.

71. Answer: c. A broker
As a real estate sales associate, you will be supervised by a broker. Sales associates cannot work for themselves or start their own brokerages. The broker is liable for the sales associate's actions.

72. Answer: b. Liable
A broker will be liable for your actions while you are performing real estate duties.

73. Answer: d. Environmental hazard
Hazardous materials have to be disposed of properly, sometimes by a specialized team.

74. Answer: a. Follow-up
Touching base with a buyer after a sale is called follow-up.

75. Answer: b. 24 hours
If a sales associate is given any money for real estate transactions, it is his/her responsibility to turn it over to the broker within 24 hours.

76. Answer: c. Open houses
Sales associates will often conduct an open house, allowing the public to tour a property without an appointment. Open houses can generate a lot of foot traffic, especially for newly listed properties.

77. Answer: d. Relationships
Building and facilitating connections in a community or sales area is an important part of a sales associate's job.

78. Answer: a. Waterfront properties
Because it is a peninsula, Florida has many waterfront properties, with laws to protect and regulate these.

79. Answer: c. 45
Sales associates are required to complete 45 hours of post-licensing education within the first 12 months after receiving their license.

80. Answer: b. 14
After the first year, sales associates are required to complete 14 hours of continued education annually.

81. Answer: d. Both B and C
Continued education allows sales associates to stay current on codes, zoning, laws and changes in licensing and continued education requirements.

82. Answer: a. Involuntary inactive
If you are working under a broker and the broker dies, your license will become involuntary inactive until you are hired under a new broker and the proper paperwork has been submitted.

83. Answer: c. Chattel
Another term for personal property is chattel.

84. Answer: d. VA loans
Specialized loans for service members are called VA loans.

85. Answer: a. 2
To transition from being a sales associate to a broker, you must have actively worked in the field for two years first.

86. Answer: a. High school diploma or GED
To be eligible to become a real estate agent, you must have a high school diploma or GED.

87. Answer: b. Originating Agency Identification
You will need an Originating Agency Identification Number (ORI) when you schedule your appointment for digital fingerprinting. Every professional agency has its own distinct ORI Number that lets agencies that are handling your information know where your data should be sent.

88. Answer: c. Florida Department of Law Enforcement's
You can find a current list of approved Live Scan providers on the Florida Department of Law Enforcement's website.

89. Answer: a. Review your application and criminal history to determine if you are still eligible to become a real estate agent
If you have a criminal history, the Florida Real Estate Commission and/or the Department of Business and Professional Regulation will review your application to determine eligibility.

90. Answer: a. Monday through Saturday
Pearson VUE has 21 testing sites that offer testing Monday through Saturday.

91. Answer: a. The day of testing
Pearson VUE will accept reservations to take the Florida Real Estate Licensing Exam up until the day of the test. Reservations can be made through Pearson VUE's customer service call center, or they can be made online via Pearson VUE's website.

92. Answer: b. Fit you in if they can
If you are late for your exam, Pearson VUE will fit you in if possible. Otherwise, your exam will be rescheduled for another day.

93. Answer: d. Major holidays
The testing center operates year-round, Monday through Saturday, except for major holidays.

94. Answer: a. Make arrangements to pay it before the exam date
If you cannot pay your exam fee at the time you register, you may make arrangements to pay it before the exam day.

95. Answer: b. A person or computer to fill the exam out
Pearson VUE allows those with disabilities to apply for accommodations to take the exam.

96. Answer: a. Provide supporting documents
In order to be approved for testing accommodations, you will be required to provide supporting documents.

97. Answer: b. As needed
Accommodations for testing will be provided on an as-needed basis.

98. Answer: b. Business casual
The dress code for exam day is business casual. The facilities are generally climate-controlled, but not always. Consider bringing a light jacket, sweatshirt or sweater.

99. Answer: b. 2
You are required to bring two forms of identification when checking in for your state exam. At least one of those must be a government-issued photo ID.

100. Answer: a. Every year
A real estate sales associate license must be renewed every year.

# Broker Practice Test 1

1. Under Title 32, Chapter 475.175 of the Florida statutes, which department or organization is responsible for receiving electronic fingerprints and background checks?
    a. The Florida Department of Law Enforcement
    b. The Florida Real Estate Commission
    c. The Florida District Attorney
    d. The Florida Board of Professional Conduct

2. Under Title 32, Chapter 475.180 of the Florida statutes, how long does a licensed broker have to inform the Florida Real Estate Commission that he/she has moved out of state?
    a. 14 days
    b. 30 days
    c. 60 days
    d. 90 days

3. Under Title 32, Chapter 475.181 of the Florida statutes, an application to take the Florida State Real Estate Exam can be on file for ____ before it expires and the individual must start the process over.
    a. 6 months
    b. 1 year
    c. 30 months
    d. 2 years

4. Under Title 32, Chapter 475.182 of the Florida statutes, any licensee who has a voluntary inactive license must complete __ hours of continued education each year in order to keep his/her license.
    a. 6
    b. 12
    c. 14
    d. 28

5. Under Florida law, all licensees must receive notice that their license is due to expire ____ before the expiration date.
    a. 30 days
    b. 60 days
    c. 90 days
    d. 120 days

6. Under Florida licensing laws, license renewals cost ____ or less each year.
    a. $25
    b. $50
    c. $75
    d. $100

7. By law, the door or front entrance of a brokerage or branch office must be furnished with:
    a. A sign bearing the brokerage name, broker's name as it appears on the license and the phrase "licensed real estate broker"
    b. The business license clearly displayed
    c. A welcome sign inviting prospective buyers and sellers inside
    d. The broker's name and phone number clearly printed

8. Under state law, which individuals are not permitted to perform real estate tasks for themselves and must work under the supervision of others?
    a. Broker associates
    b. Brokers
    c. Sales associates
    d. Both A and B

9. What topic is covered under Title 32, Chapter 475.272 of the Florida statutes?
    a. Short titles
    b. Brokerage Relationship Disclosure Act
    c. Sales and requisitions
    d. Both A and B

10. What is the ADA?
    a. The Advanced Directive Assessment
    b. The American Development Act
    c. The Americans with Disabilities Act
    d. The Arts, Décor and Accents

11. The Florida Fair Housing Act was enacted in:
    a. 1948
    b. 1958
    c. 1968
    d. 1978

12. What is the purpose of the Florida Residential Landlord and Tenant Act?
    a. To facilitate balanced and fair relationships between landlords and tenants
    b. To protect landlords from damages that are caused by tenants
    c. To protect tenants from unlawful treatment by landlords
    d. To dictate the market rates and lease terms of residential tenants

13. To maintain security deposits and advanced rental payment, landlords are given __ options to maintain the security of those funds.
    a. 2
    b. 3
    c. 4
    d. 5

14. One option a landlord has is to place funds in a separate, non-interest-bearing ____.
    a. Checking account
    b. Escrow account
    c. Personal account
    d. Home safe

15. Landlords may secure funds in a/an ____ escrow account, and the tenant will receive either 5% simple interest or 75% of actual interest earned.
    a. Non-interest-bearing
    b. Collateral-based
    c. Interest-bearing
    d. High-interest

16. By law, a landlord must maintain a property's:
    a. Normal working order
    b. Landscaping
    c. Updated fixtures
    d. Amenities

17. Normal working order includes ____, ____ and ____.
    a. Housekeeping, landscaping and curb appeal
    b. Hot water, heat and pest control
    c. Air conditioning, spa and pool
    d. Interior flooring, paint and décor

18. By state law, landlords must return the security deposit within ____ if they do not need to use any of it for damages or repairs.
    a. 7 days
    b. 15 days
    c. 30 days
    d. 45 days

19. By law, a landlord is required to notify a tenant within ____ if a security deposit is being used for repairs.
    a. 5 days
    b. 15 days
    c. 30 days
    d. 45 days

20. In the event that a landlord is in breach of a lease, the tenant has the right to follow appropriate legal channels to seek a reduction in rent or:

   a. Refuse to make any rental payments until the landlord agrees to a new lease and terms
   b. Withhold rent until the matter is resolved
   c. Ask for a refund of the security deposit
   d. Pay rent directly to the court clerk until the matter is resolved

21. What Florida law regulates the sale of parcels for the purpose of subdivisions that contain 50 or more lots?

   a. The Florida Uniform Land Sales Practices Act
   b. The Florida Rental List Law
   c. The Florida Residential Landlord and Tenant Act
   d. The Florida Environmental and Wetlands Protection Act

22. Under Title 33, Chapter 498 of the Florida statutes, what division is responsible for regulating sales pertaining to subdivisions?

   a. The Division of Real Estate
   b. The Division of Land Sales, Condominiums and Mobile Homes
   c. The Planning Commission
   d. The State Department

23. What is the Florida law that provides protection for prospective tenants who pay for a current list of rental properties if they are not able to find what they are looking for within 30 days of paying for the list?

   a. Florida disclosure law
   b. The Florida Uniform Land Sales Practices Act
   c. The Florida Rental List Law
   d. The Florida Brokers' Agreement

24. Any broker or brokerage employee who violates the Florida Do Not Call Law and solicits an individual on the no-call registry can face fines of up to:
    a. $1,000
    b. $5,000
    c. $10,000
    d. $100,000

25. One of the exemptions in the Florida Do Not Call Law, under Title 33, Chapter 500, is regarding calls made to:
    a. Other brokerages
    b. Commercial real estate
    c. Foreclosure sales
    d. Advertised "For Sale by Owner" properties

26. Calling current or former clients is not restricted or prevented by which law?
    a. The Florida Do Not Call Law
    b. The Florida Landlord and Tenant Law
    c. The Florida Rental List Law
    d. Both B and C

27. Under what Florida law were additional changes made in July 2014 pertaining to text message sales solicitation?
    a. Laws protecting confidentiality
    b. Laws protecting those on the Do Not Call list
    c. Laws regarding texting and driving
    d. Laws regarding current rental information

28. Under Florida law, anyone who pays for a current rental list and is provided with inaccurate or outdated information is entitled to a full refund within __ days from the time the property was purchased.
   a. 10
   b. 14
   c. 30
   d. 60

29. Under the Florida Rental List Law, anyone who purchases a rental list and is unable to find the property he/she is looking for within 30 days may be entitled to a refund of up to ____ of the list cost.
   a. 25%
   b. 50%
   c. 75%
   d. 90%

30. Violations of the Florida Rental List Law may result in fines of ____ or less, up to ____ in jail, or both, with the possibility of a first-degree misdemeanor charge.
   a. $1,000, one year
   b. $500, five years
   c. $1,000, three years
   d. $10,000, one year

31. Under which type of Florida law are sales associates and brokers required to inform potential buyers of structural issues, infestations, natural organisms, flooding, roofing and other system damages or issues the property may have?
   a. The Fair Housing Act
   b. Disclosure laws
   c. Flood insurance laws
   d. Title insurance laws

32. Which of the following does not have to be disclosed to potential buyers in regard to a property on the market?
    a. Property stigmas
    b. Previous ownership
    c. Tangible property deficits or damage
    d. Property erosion information

33. Information on new residential builds is considered assumed knowledge for the property situation and, therefore, is not part of the protections under which of the following laws?
    a. Florida Tenant and Landlord Law
    b. Florida Disclosure Law
    c. Florida Homestead Act
    d. Florida Green Belt Law

34. Under Title 32, Chapter 475 of the Florida statutes, the Financial Institutions Reform, Recovery and Enforcement Act (FIRREA) was established in which of the following years?
    a. 1969
    b. 1979
    c. 1989
    d. 1999

35. As per the Financial Institutions Reform, Recovery and Enforcement Act, all properties are required to have a/an ____ before a sale or purchase can be made.
    a. Contract
    b. Deed
    c. Appraisal
    d. Inspection

36. Qualified appraisers must be educated and licensed under the universal standard of professional appraisal practices in order to legally perform which of the following actions under the Financial Institutions Reform, Recovery and Enforcement Act of 1989?
    a. Comparative market analysis
    b. Relative market comparisons
    c. Fair market value listings
    d. Official property appraisals
37. In order to legally conduct an appraisal and provide a legally binding appraisal report in the State of Florida, an individual must be a/an ____ or ____.
    a. Appraiser or appraisal broker
    b. Sales associate or broker
    c. Broker associate or broker
    d. Lender or borrower

38. The Florida Homestead Act pertains to which of the following?
    a. Tax exemption
    b. Special tax
    c. Personal property tax
    d. Tax liability

39. Tax exemptions for the sale of an individual's primary residence are granted under which of the following laws?
    a. The Florida Green Belt Law
    b. The Florida Homestead Act
    c. The Florida Fair Housing Act
    d. Florida foreclosure law

40. The Florida Homestead Act may allow tax exemptions between ___ and ___.

a. $10,000 and $30,000
b. $20,000 and $50,000
c. $25,000 and $75,000
d. $50,000 and $100,000

41. In order to qualify for the Florida Homestead Act tax exemption, you must file the proper documents through which of the following state offices?

a. The county assessor's office
b. The Department of Real Estate
c. The Internal Revenue Service
d. The Florida Department of Revenue

42. Tax credits, tax exemptions and tax breaks are offered to agricultural property owners under which of the following Florida laws?

a. The Green Belt Law
b. The Florida Homestead Act
c. The Community Planning Act
d. The Environmental Protection Act

43. The Florida Green Belt Law assesses the value of a given property based on its ____ rather than its actual value, which generally provides the property with a lower overall value, qualifying the property for lower taxes.

a. Zoning
b. Agricultural purposes
c. Fair market value
d. Businesses generation

44. In order to receive exemptions, tax breaks or lower property taxes under the Green Belt Law, property owners must apply ____ for these incentives.

   a. Monthly
   b. Semiannually
   c. Annually
   d. As needed

45. Under which Florida law are you legally required to have contracts and agreements prepared in written form in order for a court of law to consider the documents valid?

   a. Fair credit laws
   b. Foreclosure laws
   c. Fair housing laws
   d. Statute of frauds

46. Greg is putting in a barn on the back corner of his property. The barn is 28 feet wide and 28 feet long. What is the area of Greg's barn?

   a. 630 square feet
   b. 784 square feet
   c. 820 square feet
   d. 960 square feet

47. Gavin purchases a condo with a down payment of $22,000 and a mortgage of $478,000 at an interest rate of 12% for a 15-year term. The monthly payments are $2,660. What is the loan-to-value ratio?

   a. 1.29
   b. 1.00
   c. 0.96
   d. 0.68

48. Ben's Boxing Gym rents for $45 per square foot with an index of 6.8. The index increases to 7.4. What is the adjustable rental rate?

a. $46.97
b. $47.97
c. $49.05
d. $49.97

49. The Surf Shop by the Bay rents for $62 per square foot with an index of 9.8. The index increases to 10.4. What is the adjustable rental rate?

a. $65.80
b. $62.80
c. $26.27
d. $65.79

50. The roller rink rents for $12 a square foot with an index of 0.4. The index increases to 0.8. What is the adjustable rental rate?

a. $20.00
b. $22.00
c. $24.00
d. $26.00

51. The motorcycle shop rents for $9 a square foot with an index of 1.6. The index increases to 4.3. What is the adjustable rental rate?

a. $24.18
b. $24.19
c. $34.19
d. $44.19

52. Derick has an estimated monthly housing expense of $520, and his monthly obligations total $2,200. If Derick has a monthly gross income of $3,010, what is the total obligations ratio?
    a. 33%
    b. 53%
    c. 73%
    d. 93%

53. Adam has an estimated monthly housing expense of $965, and his monthly obligations total $1,600. If Adam has a monthly gross income of $3,200, what is the total obligations ratio?
    a. 20%
    b. 30%
    c. 40%
    d. 50%

54. Kelsey applies for a 30-year mortgage of $360,200 at 4.5% interest. How much of the $1,000 monthly payment paid in the second month will apply to the principal?
    a. -$352.07
    b. $1,352.07
    c. $352.07
    d. $3,520.70

55. Jenna moves into her college apartment in mid-August. She signs a lease on August 18. The rent for the apartment is $320 a month. The landlord will prorate the rent for the month of August, and Jenna will pay for only the days she is actually living in the apartment from August 18 to 31, not including the day she signs the lease. What is Jenna's prorated rent for August?

    a. $144.52
    b. $134.19
    c. $44.52
    d. $414.52

56. In order to meet the prerequisites to take your Florida Real Estate Exam for Brokers, you are required to work as a sales associate for a minimum of how many years over a five-year period?

    a. 1 year
    b. 2 years
    c. 3 years
    d. 4 years

57. Sales associates who wish to become real estate brokers in the State of Florida are required to complete a ___-hour pre-licensing education course before they can apply to take the state exam.

    a. 12
    b. 14
    c. 64
    d. 72

58. To pass the pre-licensing education course for brokers, you must complete all of the required class hours and pass the exam at the end of the course with a minimum of what percentage?

   a. 70%
   b. 75%
   c. 80%
   d. 90%

59. After getting your broker's license, you are required to complete post-licensing education courses within how many months of first receiving your license?

   a. 6 months
   b. 9 months
   c. 12 months
   d. 24 months

60. What is the required number of hours a broker must complete of continued education each year before his/her license can be renewed?

   a. 12 hours
   b. 14 hours
   c. 16 hours
   d. 18 hours

61. A principle or main office is required to be maintained by which of the following individuals?

   a. Real estate appraisers
   b. Real estate sales associates
   c. Real estate brokers
   d. Real estate brokerages

62. All brokers are required to have a sign on their front door or near the entrance that displays the brokerage name, if there is one, as well as which two of the following?
    a. The office address and phone number
    b. The names of sales associates and brokerage associates who work under the broker
    c. The hours of operation and contact information
    d. The broker's name as it appears on his/her license and the words "licensed real estate broker"

63. A broker may choose to do all of the following except ____ when it comes to the office that he/she works out of.
    a. Establish a home office
    b. Work at a brokerage with other brokers
    c. Start his/her own brokerage
    d. Forgo having an office in order to be mobile

64. If you decide to start a brokerage, which of the following is an essential first step to take?
    a. Generate capital to start your brokerage
    b. Develop a business plan and determine the overall start-up cost
    c. Find investors to assist you with the capital to start your brokerage
    d. Rent or purchase a property for your office

65. As a broker, you will be liable for which of the following?
    a. Your actions
    b. Your actions and the actions of the sales associates who work under your supervision
    c. The actions of your clients
    d. The actions of lenders that finance you or your clients

66. Before contracting any sales associates to work under your supervision, it is important to do which of the following?
    a. Develop an application and screening process for prospective employees
    b. Develop policies and procedures for how you will conduct business and handle disciplinary matters
    c. Develop a contract for those who will work with you or under your supervision
    d. All of the above

67. It is the responsibility of which of the following parties to ensure that the Florida Real Estate Commission's guidelines, the Department of Business and Professional Regulation's codes of conduct, and local, state and federal laws are followed?
    a. Office manager
    b. Sales associate
    c. Broker
    d. General manager

68. To protect financial assets, it is important for a broker to have a/an:
    a. Office safe
    b. Stock portfolio
    c. Money market account
    d. Escrow account

69. A broker is required to deposit funds for safekeeping within how many days of receiving them?
    a. 1 day
    b. 3 days
    c. 5 days
    d. 7 days

70. The sales associates who work under your supervision may receive deposits for various transactions that they undertake in your name. Sales associates are required to get those funds to you, the broker, within what amount of time?

   a. 24 hours
   b. 48 hours
   c. 36 hours
   d. 72 hours

71. A broker must maintain complete records to ensure that they are ready for which of the following events?

   a. IRS audit
   b. Better Business Bureau
   c. Routine inspection
   d. Division of Real Estate

72. A routine inspection can be conducted at which of the following times?

   a. After hours
   b. At reasonable times during regular business hours
   c. Before the business is open for the day
   d. Any time a monitoring agency feels it is necessary

73. The Department of Business and Professional Regulation audits which of the following?

   a. Health and safety codes
   b. Sales associates
   c. A broker's escrow accounts
   d. An office's cleanliness and presentability

74. Bank statements, reconciliation bank statements, canceled checks, deposit slips, monthly reconciliations, liabilities, bank balance information and interest-bearing accounts will all be reviewed during:
    a. An audit by the Department of Business and Professional Regulation
    b. A code inspection by a city or county building inspector
    c. Renewal of your broker's license each year
    d. None of the above

75. In the event that minor discrepancies are found in your records during an audit, the Department of Business and Professional Regulation will issue you which of the following?
    a. A subpoena
    b. A notice of noncompliance
    c. A cease-and-desist order
    d. A citation

76. In the event that a complaint is filed with the Florida Real Estate Commission, which of the following actions will occur first?
    a. License suspension
    b. Fines levied
    c. An investigation
    d. Licensure being completely revoked

77. A broker has the right to request what action after the Florida Real Estate Commission issues its final order regarding a complaint?
    a. Appeal
    b. Contest
    c. Argue
    d. Dismiss

78. Without taking the matter to court, penalties for minor violations can include all of the following actions except:

   a. Suspension or revocation of your real estate license
   b. Fines not to exceed $5,000
   c. Disciplinary probation
   d. Jail time

79. Unless they possess the specialized license to do so, brokers are not permitted to do which of the following activities?

   a. Comparative market analyses
   b. Appraisals
   c. Fair market assessments
   d. Current market reveals

80. As a broker, helping an individual or entity sell a business will require you to conduct which of the following activities?

   a. Comparative market analysis
   b. Property valuation
   c. Business valuation
   d. Commission

81. Purchase contracts, listing agreements, buyer broker agreements and options contracts are:

   a. Record-keeping
   b. Closing documents
   c. Comparative market analysis components
   d. Four types of arrangements commonly handled

82. As a broker, you can expect a fee between ____ and ____ when you are managing properties or investments.
   a. 10% and 50%
   b. 20% and 40%
   c. 30% and 60%
   d. 40% and 80%

83. If your brokerage focuses on sales in a specific area and you familiarize yourself with that area to ensure that prospective buyers get the best information possible, this is known as:
   a. Valuation
   b. Farm area
   c. Blockbusting
   d. Redlining

84. A parcel refers to which kind of real estate?
   a. A piece of land
   b. A condominium
   c. A house
   d. An industrial property

85. Properties such as homes, townhomes and duplexes are the bulk of what makes up the total properties in an area. This is known as a _______ area.
   a. Industrial
   b. Residential
   c. Commercial
   d. Special use

86. Main Street in the center of town (with stores, shops, pharmacies, a bookstore and a laundromat) is an example of which type of property?
   a. Residential
   b. Special use
   c. Agricultural
   d. Commercial

87. A strip of land outside of town that is occupied by factories and production plants is an example of which type of property?
   a. Industrial
   b. Agricultural
   c. Commercial
   d. Special use

88. As a broker, part of your job will most likely include property management. Property managers handle the bulk of which of the following activities?
   a. Day-to-day operations
   b. Showing and leasing rentals
   c. Maintaining and inspecting the property
   d. A, B and C

89. Good-quality tenants are essential for:
   a. Rental properties
   b. Investment properties
   c. Property sales
   d. Purchasing properties

90. Fixed, graduated, ground, net, percentage and gross are the six types of:
   a. Fixtures
   b. Leases
   c. Escrow accounts
   d. Closings

91. When you manage a property that is owned by an individual who does not reside on the premises, the individual is a/an:
   a. Absentee owner
   b. Property owner
   c. Landlord
   d. Agent

92. It is a second-degree misdemeanor for a broker to project false or misleading information to the public. This is known as:
   a. Liability
   b. False advertising
   c. Deception
   d. Depreciation

93. If a licensed real estate agent sells his/her own property as "For Sale by Owner," the agent should disclose what information before beginning negotiations or proceeding with contracts?
   a. Personal contact information
   b. A chain of title
   c. Real estate license
   d. Constructive notice

94. As a broker, if you use email advertising, you are required to provide a/an ____ option for people who do not want to keep being solicited.
   a. Subscription
   b. Purchase
   c. Opt-out
   d. None of the above

95. The Florida Commercial Bank, Florida Credit Union and the Florida Savings and Loan Association are all examples of:
   a. Mortgage lenders
   b. Property managers
   c. Lienholders
   d. Acceptable depositories

96. Buyers should be instructed to write checks payable to which of the following?
   a. The associate handling the closing
   b. The point of contact at the brokerage
   c. The broker's escrow account
   d. The associate's personal account

97. For an escrow account to be broker-held, the broker must:
   a. Have his/her own personal escrow account
   b. Be a signatory on the escrow account
   c. Be able to deposit funds in the escrow account
   d. None of the above

98. Brokers need written permission from all parties when depositing funds into what type of account?

   a. An interest-bearing escrow account
   b. An escrow account
   c. A money market account
   d. An investment portfolio

99. In notice and settlement procedures, brokers are not allowed to do which of the following actions without the agreement of all parties?

   a. Dispute escrow funds
   b. Deposit escrow funds
   c. Comingle escrow funds
   d. Withdraw escrow funds

100. What is required before binding arbitration can be executed?

   a. Prior consent of all parties
   b. Concurrency
   c. Cooperative judgment
   d. Jury of peers

# Answers – Broker Practice Test 1

1. Answer: a. The Florida Department of Law Enforcement
   The Florida Department of Law Enforcement is responsible for receiving electronic fingerprints and background checks.

2. Answer: c. 60 days
   Under Title 32, Chapter 475.180 of the Florida statutes, a licensed individual must inform the Florida Real Estate Commission within 60 days if he/she moves out of state.

3. Answer: d. 2 years
   Under Title 32, Chapter 475.181 of the Florida statutes, an application to take the Florida State Real Estate Licensing Exam can be on file for two years before it expires.

4. Answer: c. 14
   Under Title 32, Chapter 475.182 of the Florida statutes, any licensee who has a voluntary inactive license must complete 14 hours of continued education each year.

5. Answer: c. 90 days
   Under Florida law, all licensees will receive notice that their license is due to expire 90 days before the expiration date.

6. Answer: d. $100
   Under Florida licensing laws, license renewals cost $100 or less each year.

7. Answer: a. A sign bearing the brokerage name, broker's name as it appears on the license and the phrase "licensed real estate broker"
   By law, the door or front entrance of a brokerage or branch office must be furnished with all of the above details.

8. Answer: c. Sales associates
   Under Florida law, sales associates are required to work under the supervision of a licensed real estate broker.

9. Answer: d. Both A and B
   Title 32, Chapter 475.272 of the Florida statutes covers the Brokerage Relationship Disclosure Act as well as short titles.

10. Answer: c. The Americans with Disabilities Act
    The acronym ADA stands for the Americans with Disabilities Act.

11. Answer: c. 1968
    The Florida Fair Housing Act was enacted in 1968.

12. Answer: a. To facilitate balanced and fair relationships between landlords and tenants
    The Florida Residential Landlord and Tenant Act facilitates balanced and fair relationships between landlords and tenants.

13. Answer: b. 3
    Landlords are given three options to maintain security deposits and advanced rental payments.

14. Answer: b. Escrow account
    One option a landlord has is to place funds in a separate, non-interest-bearing escrow account.

15. Answer: c. Interest-bearing
    Landlords may secure funds in an interest-bearing escrow account, and the tenant will receive either 5% simple interest or 75% of actual interest earned.

16. Answer: a. Normal working order
    By law, a landlord must maintain his/her properties and keep things in normal working order.

17. Answer: b. Hot water, heat and pest control
    Normal working order includes hot water, heat and pest control.

18. Answer: b. 15 days
    By state law, a landlord must return a security deposit within 15 days if it is not needed to pay for damages or repairs.

19. Answer: c. 30 days
    By law, a landlord is required to notify a tenant within 30 days if a security deposit is being used for repairs.

20. Answer: d. Pay rent directly to the court clerk until the matter is resolved
    In the event that a landlord is in breach of a lease, the tenant has the right to follow appropriate legal channels to seek a reduction in rent or pay rent directly to the court clerk until the matter is resolved.

21. Answer: a. Florida Uniform Land Sales Practices Act
The Florida Uniform Land Sales Practices Act regulates the sale of parcels for the purpose of subdivisions that contain 50 or more lots.

22. Answer: b. The Division of Land Sales, Condominiums and Mobile Homes
Under Title 33, Chapter 498 of the Florida statutes, the Division of Land Sales, Condominiums and Mobile Homes is responsible for regulating sales pertaining to subdivisions.

23. Answer: c. The Florida Rental List Law
The Florida Rental List Law provides assorted protections for prospective tenants.

24. Answer: c. $10,000
Any broker or brokerage employee who violates the Florida Do Not Call Law can face fines of up to $10,000.

25. Answer: d. Advertised "For Sale by Owner" properties
One of the exemptions in the Florida Do Not Call Law is regarding calls made to advertise "For Sale by Owner" properties.

26. Answer: a. The Florida Do Not Call Law
Calling current or former clients is not restricted or prevented by the Florida Do Not Call Law.

27. Answer: b. Laws protecting those on the Do Not Call list
Additional changes were made in July 2014 pertaining to text message sales solicitation.

28. Answer: c. 30

Under Florida law, anyone who pays for a current rental list and is provided with inaccurate or outdated information is entitled to a full refund within 30 days from the time the list was purchased.

29. Answer: c. 75%

Under the Florida Rental List Law, anyone who purchases a rental list and is unable to find the property he/she is looking for within 30 days may be entitled to a refund of up to 75% of the list cost.

30. Answer: a. $1,000, one year

Violations to the Florida Rental List Law may result in fines of $1,000 or less, up to one year in jail, or both, with the possibility of a first-degree misdemeanor charge.

31. Answer: b. Disclosure laws

Under the Florida Disclosure Law, sales associates and brokers are required to inform potential buyers of any problems the property they are seeking to purchase may have.

32. Answer: a. Property stigmas

Brokers, broker associates and sales associates do not have to disclose property stigmas, such as deaths, murders, or illnesses, to potential buyers under the Florida Disclosure Law.

33. Answer: b. Florida Disclosure Law

Information on new residential builds is considered assumed knowledge and, therefore, is not part of the protections under the Florida Disclosure Law.

34. Answer: c. 1989
The Financial Institutions Reform, Recovery and Enforcement Act was established in 1989.

35. Answer: c. Appraisal
Under the Financial Institutions Reform, Recovery and Enforcement Act of 1989, all real estate properties are required to have an appraisal before a sale or purchase can be made.

36. Answer: d. Official property appraisals
Qualified appraisers must be educated and licensed under the universal standard of professional appraisal practices.

37. Answer: a. Appraiser or appraisal broker
In order to legally conduct an appraisal and provide a legally binding appraisal report in the State of Florida, an individual must be an appraiser or appraisal broker.

38. Answer: a. Tax exemption
The Florida Homestead Act pertains to tax exemptions on real estate properties, specifically in purchasing homes.

39. Answer: b. The Florida Homestead Act
Tax exemptions for the sale of an individual's primary residence are granted under the Florida Homestead Act.

40. Answer: c. $25,000 and $75,000
The Florida Homestead Act may allow tax exemptions between $25,000 and $75,000.

41. Answer: d. The Florida Department of Revenue
In order to qualify for the Florida Homestead Act tax exemption, you must file the proper documents through the Florida Department of Revenue.

42. Answer: a. The Green Belt Law
Tax credits, tax exemptions and tax breaks are offered to agricultural property owners under the Green Belt Law.

43. Answer: b. Agricultural purposes
The Florida Green Belt Law assesses the value of a given property based on its agricultural purposes rather than its actual value, resulting in lower property taxes.

44. Answer: c. Annually
In order to receive exemptions, tax breaks or lower property taxes under the Green Belt Law, property owners must apply annually for these incentives.

45. Answer: d. Statute of frauds
Under Florida law, contracts and agreements are legally required to be in writing in order to be considered valid.

46. Answer: b. 784 square feet
Greg's barn will have a total area of 784 square feet.

47. Answer: c. 0.96
Gavin will have a loan-to-value ratio of 0.96 for his condo.

48. Answer: d. $49.97
The adjustable rent rate for Ben's Boxing Gym will be $49.97.

49. Answer: a. $65.80
The Surf Shop by the Bay will have an adjustable rent rate of $65.80, rounded to the nearest cent.

50. Answer: c. $24.00
The adjustable rental rate for the roller rink will be $24.00.

51. Answer: b. $24.19
The adjustable rental rate for the motorcycle shop will be $24.19.

52. Answer: c. 73%
Derick will have a total obligations ratio of 73%.

53. Answer: d. 50%
The total obligations ratio for Adam is 50%.

54. Answer: a. -$352.07
-$352.07 of the $1,000 monthly payment will apply to the principal.

55. Answer: b. $134.19
The prorated rent for August will be $134.19.

56. Answer: b. 2 years
In order to meet the prerequisites to take your Florida Real Estate Exam for Brokers, you are required to work as a sales associate for a minimum of two years over a five-year period.

57. Answer: d. 72
Sales associates who wish to become real estate brokers in the State of Florida are required to complete a 72-hour pre-licensing education course first.

58. Answer: b. 75%
To pass the pre-licensing education course for brokers, you must complete all of the required class hours and pass the exam at the end of the course with a minimum of 75%.

59. Answer: c. 12 months
After getting your broker's license, you are required to complete a post-licensing education course within the first 12 months of getting your broker's license.

60. Answer: b. 14 hours
Brokers must complete 14 hours of continued education each year.

61. Answer: c. Real estate brokers
A principle or main office is required to be maintained by all real estate brokers.

62. Answer: d. The broker's name as it appears on his/her license and the words "licensed real estate broker"
All brokers are required to have a sign on their front door or near the entrance that contains all of the above information.

63. Answer: d. Forgo having an office in order to be mobile
By Florida state law, a broker *must* have an office. It may be a home office, a broker may choose to work with others at a brokerage firm, or he/she may start his/her own brokerage, but the business must have a main office.

64. Answer: b. Develop a business plan and determine the overall start-up cost
If you decide to start a brokerage, you must first determine the overall start-up cost.

65. Answer: b. Your actions and the actions of the sales associates who work under your supervision
As a broker, you will be liable for your actions and the actions of the sales associates who work under your supervision, along with any non-licensed employees you hire.

66. Answer: d. All of the above
You must develop an application and screening process for prospective employees and contractors, develop policies and procedures for how you will conduct business and handle disciplinary matters, and develop a contract for those who will work with you or under your supervision before hiring employees.

67. Answer: c. Broker
It is the responsibility of brokers to ensure that the Florida Real Estate Commission guidelines, the Department of Business and Professional Regulation's codes of conduct, and local, state and federal laws are followed.

68. Answer: d. Escrow account
To protect financial assets, a broker should establish an escrow account.

69. Answer: b. 3 days
A broker is required to deposit funds for safekeeping within three business days of receiving them.

70. Answer: a. 24 hours
Sales associates are required to get funds to the broker within 24 hours of receiving them. They should also ensure that any checks are made out to the brokerage or broker's escrow account.

71. Answer: c. Routine inspection
A broker must maintain thorough records to ensure that the business is prepared for any routine inspections.

72. Answer: b. At reasonable times during regular business hours
The Florida Real Estate Commission and the Department of Business and Professional Regulation may conduct an inspection, without notice, at any reasonable time during regular business hours.

73. Answer: c. A broker's escrow accounts
The Department of Business and Professional Regulation will audit escrow accounts held by brokers and brokerages.

74. Answer: a. An audit by the Department of Business and Professional Regulation
During an audit, the Department of Business and Professional Regulation will review bank statements, reconciliation bank statements, canceled checks, deposit slips, monthly reconciliations, liabilities, bank balance information and interest-bearing accounts.

75. Answer: b. A notice of noncompliance
In the event that minor discrepancies are found during an audit, the Department of Business and Professional Regulation will issue a broker or brokerage with a notice of noncompliance. The real estate agent or brokerage will then have a brief window to rectify the situation.

76. Answer: c. An investigation
In the event that a complaint is filed with the Florida Real Estate Commission, the first step taken will be an investigation to determine if there is enough evidence to move forward with complaint proceedings.

77. Answer: a. Appeal
A broker has the right to request an appeal after the Florida Real Estate Commission issues its final order regarding a complaint.

78. Answer: d. Jail time
If misconduct is made on the part of a real estate agent, minor matters will be taken before the Florida Real Estate Commission. However, more severe violations will be taken to a court of law, where violators can expect to have hefty fines levied against them or to even serve jail time.

79. Answer: b. Appraisals
Unless they possess the specialized license to do so, brokers are not permitted to conduct appraisals. A Florida licensed appraiser or a broker appraiser are the only individuals who can legally conduct appraisals and produce an official appraisal report.

80. Answer: c. Business valuation
As a broker, helping an individual or entity sell a business will require you to conduct a thorough business valuation.

81. Answer: d. Four types of arrangements commonly handled
As a real estate agent, you will most commonly be handling purchase contracts, listing agreements, buyer broker agreements and options contracts.

82. Answer: a. 10% and 50%
As a broker, you can expect a fee between 10% and 50% when you are managing both rental and investment properties. The type of property you manage and its size will both play a part in negotiating and determining that percentage.

83. Answer: b. Farm area
Much like a farmer, you are familiar with the property and know it quite well.

84. Answer: a. A piece of land
A parcel refers to a vacant piece of land.

85. Answer: b. Residential
Property such as homes, townhomes and duplexes are known as residential property and would be located in a residential area.

86. Answer: d. Commercial
Commercial properties are generally used by businesses.

87. Answer: a. Industrial
A strip of land outside of town that is occupied by factories is known as industrial property.

88. Answer: d. A, B and C
As a real estate agent, when you are managing properties, it is common for you to be responsible for the day-to-day operations, show the property to prospective tenants, lease the property, schedule maintenance, take care of the general upkeep and conduct property inspections.

89. Answer: a. Rental properties
Good-quality tenants ensure that the property will be respected and cared for. These types of tenants are also more likely to recommend your property to others in their social circles.

90. Answer: b. Leases
There are six types of leases that you will generally see as a real estate agent: fixed lease, graduated lease, ground lease, net lease, percentage lease and gross lease.

91. Answer: a. Absentee owner
    Absentee owners refer to a property owner who does not live on the property, but rents the property out, and the property is either managed by a real estate company or by an off-site manager.

92. Answer: b. False advertising
    Sales associates, brokers and brokerages face a second-degree charge if they are found guilty of false advertising. Such actions can include misrepresenting the brokerage, embellishing the truth, exaggerating in advertising or outright lying.

93. Answer: c. Real estate license
    When a real estate agent is selling his/her own property as "For Sale by Owner" and will be representing him/herself during the transaction, that information should be shared with prospective buyers before starting any negotiations or contracts.

94. Answer: c. Opt-out
    As a broker, if you use email advertising, you are required to provide an opt-out option for those who do not want to continue receiving solicitation.

95. Answer: d. Acceptable depositories
    The Florida Commercial Bank, Florida Credit Union and the Florida Savings and Loan Association are all acceptable depositories for brokers to use when handling funds.

96. Answer: c. The broker's escrow account
Buyers should be instructed to write checks payable to the broker's escrow account. This is especially true when business is being conducted by someone other than the broker.

97. Answer: b. Be a signatory on the escrow account
For an escrow account to be broker-held, the broker must be a signatory on that account.

98. Answer: a. An interest-bearing escrow account
Before funds may be deposited, brokers need written permission from all parties involved if they use an interest-bearing escrow account.

99. Answer: a. Dispute escrow funds
In order to dispute escrow funds, a broker must have the consent of all parties involved.

100. Answer: a. Prior consent of all parties
Prior consent from all parties is required before binding arbitration can be executed.

# Broker Practice Test 2

1. When a broker has no financial claim in a legal matter, the broker is known as a/an:
    a. Interpleader
    b. Mediator
    c. Negotiator
    d. Property manager

2. While the real estate commission issues a determination of who is entitled to disputed funds, funds must be held in a brokerage escrow account. The Florida Real Estate Commission must be informed within 10 business days if the dispute is settled. This settlement is known as:
    a. Good faith doubt
    b. Escrow disbursement order
    c. Summary judgment
    d. Notice of settlement

3. When a broker doubts the intentions of either party to act in good faith according to the contract between the parties, this is known as:
    a. Probable cause
    b. Exculpatory clause
    c. Good faith doubt
    d. Contract rescinded

4. Who determines a broker's commission in the State of Florida?
    a. The State of Florida regulates commissions
    b. Brokers negotiate their own commissions
    c. The Florida Real Estate Commission regulates commissions
    d. The Division of Real Estate regulates commissions

5. Anyone who is a general partner, officer or director of a brokerage partnership or corporation is encompassed under which of the following titles?
   a. Broker associate
   b. Sales associate
   c. Broker
   d. Appraiser

6. If a broker is the only owner in the business, holds full liability for the business, retains an active broker's license and has a business registered under either his/her own name or a trade name, this business is known as a:
   a. Limited liability company
   b. Limited liability partnership
   c. Sole proprietorship
   d. Partnership

7. A sole proprietorship, general partnership, limited partnership, limited liability partnership, corporation and limited liability company are all business entities that may do which of the following?
   a. Register as a real estate broker
   b. Run a brokerage
   c. Sell real estate in Florida
   d. Be property managers

8. If you register as a partnership with the Department of Business and Professional Regulation and have at least one partner who is an active broker, this is known as what kind of real estate brokerage?
   a. A real estate brokerage general partnership
   b. A real estate brokerage company
   c. A real estate brokerage limited liability company
   d. A real estate brokerage corporation

9. When a broker uses a business name that is separate from his/her personal legal name, this practice is known as:
    a. False advertising
    b. Trade name
    c. Trademark
    d. Temporary broker

10. The Florida Real Estate Broker's Exam is administered:
    a. Through an electronic testing system
    b. Through a booklet and answer-sheet system
    c. Through an essay assessment
    d. Through a physical display of practical knowledge

11. When a broker is contracted to sell a property and that property owner gives the broker the sole right to sell it, this is known as:
    a. Right to sell
    b. Exclusive listing agent
    c. Open listing
    d. Net listing

12. It is not uncommon for a broker to hire a ______ to handle more routine responsibilities, such as answering phones, filing paperwork and scheduling appointments.
    a. Sales manager
    b. Personal assistant
    c. Marketing manager
    d. District manager

13. To run your brokerage smoothly, it is a good idea to compile which of the following items for all employees to know and review?
    a. A legal reference guide
    b. Real estate commission bylaws
    c. A policy manual
    d. A mission statement

14. Monthly cash receipts, a disbursement journal, a master journal, a monthly reconciliation statement, individual customer ledger sheets and a master customer ledger are all components needed for which of the following tasks?
    a. Record-keeping
    b. Financing
    c. Reconciliation
    d. Credit checks

15. Which of the following terms refers to resolving an issue in a way that is non-binding?
    a. Litigation
    b. Arbitration
    c. Escrow disbursement order
    d. Mediation

16. Once an audit is done on a broker's escrow account, the results will be discussed with the broker in which of the following time frames?
    a. 24 to 48 hours
    b. 7 to 10 days
    c. Immediately
    d. Within 30 days

17. How many steps are in the Florida Real Estate Commission's disciplinary process?
    a. 3
    b. 5
    c. 7
    d. 9

18. When listing a property, a broker uses which of the following practices to help clients come to a fair list price?
    a. Official appraisal
    b. Property valuation
    c. Capital gains
    d. Comparative market analysis

19. Investment value, assessed value, liquidation value, salvage value, insurable value and market value are all examples of which of the following terms?
    a. Types of investments
    b. Zoning codes
    c. Appraisal values
    d. Real estate options

20. The following are steps brokers take: define the problem, preliminary analysis, highest- and best-use analysis, land value estimate, application of three approaches to value, reconciliation report of value. These steps help a client understand which of the following processes?
    a. The appraisal process
    b. The marketing process
    c. The property inspection process
    d. The buying process

21. Data collection for comparable properties, adjustment of the comparable sales price and reconciliation of the adjusted sales price are the three steps in which of the following processes?
    a. Gross market analysis
    b. Sales comparison approach
    c. Property valuation analysis
    d. Liquidation value determinant

22. Conditions of sale, adjusting for financing terms and adjusting for market conditions are the three steps in which of the following options?
    a. Fair market valuation
    b. Fair market value
    c. Transactional characteristics
    d. Marketing statistics

23. The cost depreciation approach has how many steps to the process?
    a. 2 steps
    b. 4 steps
    c. 5 steps
    d. 7 steps

24. Conducting a comparative market analysis evaluating properties sold over the past 12 months, evaluating the current for-sale market and evaluating listings that expired in the past year are all types of what?
    a. Associations
    b. Comparables
    c. Competition
    d. Elements

25. To be successful as a real estate broker, you need to put effort into which of the following?
    a. Building community relationships
    b. Continuing your education
    c. Selling lucrative properties
    d. Fostering creativity

26. When conducting a business valuation, two of the most important statements you will need to have on hand are ____ and ____.
    a. Purchases and sales
    b. Assets and liabilities
    c. Balance sheets and income statements
    d. Bank statements and credit statements

27. Comparable sales approach, cost appreciation approach, income capitalization approach and liquidation value approach are all examples of:
    a. Integrated asset evaluation
    b. Charitable contributions
    c. Profits and losses
    d. Valuation approaches

28. As a broker, if you are representing a client as a single agent, the State of Florida requires you to provide which of the following to your client?
    a. Single agent notice
    b. No brokerage relationship notice
    c. Notice of non-compete
    d. Consent to transition to transaction broker

29. When a real estate broker acts as the agent for both parties in a transaction, this person is known as a:
    a. Transaction broker
    b. Dual agent
    c. Single agent
    d. Universal agent

30. In the State of Florida, real estate agents are allowed to prepare sale and purchase contracts, listing agreements, buyer broker agreements and options contracts without committing which of the following?
    a. Unlawful transactions under their license
    b. Fraudulent transactions under someone else's license
    c. Unauthorized practice of law
    d. Invalid purchases or sales

31. If possible, brokers need any documents pertaining to the properties they are preparing to sell, including but not limited to title insurance documents, survey documents and mortgage documents. Another relevant document brokers might need is a/an:
    a. Listing agreement
    b. Sale and purchase agreement
    c. Earnest money deposit
    d. Disclosure agreement

32. For homes built before 1978, brokers and sales associates must provide potential buyers with an environmental protection agency pamphlet regarding what hazard?
    a. Radon gas
    b. Lead-based paint
    c. Property stigmas
    d. HIV disclosure

33. Brokers help facilitate the matching of investments to investors. The first step for a broker in preparing to find an appropriate investment property is:
    a. Comparative market analysis
    b. Property valuation
    c. Business valuation
    d. Client evaluation

34. When a broker or landlord offers a tenant free rent, delayed rent, moving expenses or a lease buyout, these are all examples of:
    a. Depreciation
    b. Rent concession
    c. Discount point
    d. Proration

35. If a tenant is in breach of a lease and has not paid rent, a broker acting as a property manager or the landlord may issue which of the following documents to demand payment or that the tenant vacate the premises?
    a. Three-day notice
    b. Writ of possession
    c. Eviction
    d. Notice of noncompliance

36. When a tenant pays rent based on an index that has already been set, this is referred to as which of the following?
    a. A variable lease
    b. A month-to-month lease
    c. A sliding scale
    d. A unilateral contract

37. During the closing when the borrower has an FHA loan and must pay the insurance premium in one lump sum, this is known as which of the following?
    a. A down payment
    b. An upfront mortgage insurance premium
    c. Earnest money
    d. A variable lease

38. A document that is proof of ownership is known as which of the following?
    a. A contract
    b. A deed
    c. A title
    d. A bill of sale

39. Bill is a tenant in one of the properties you manage. He is leaving to take a job in another state. He makes an agreement with Hannah for her to take over the rent and utilities and live in his apartment until his lease is up. This arrangement is known as which of the following?
    a. Lease
    b. Property transfer
    c. Sublease
    d. Unilateral contract

40. What is subject property?
    a. A property that is up for auction
    b. The property you are trying to sell
    c. A piece of property that is used by the city
    d. A property that is under appraisal or potentially going to be under contract

41. A sales associate must work under the supervision of a broker or which of the following parties?
    a. A landlord
    b. A developer
    c. A lender
    d. A borrower

42. BAR SALE is another name for which of the following?
    a. Remodeling and construction
    b. Real estate services
    c. Comparative market analysis
    d. Commercial properties

43. Hotels, motels and other facilities that are used and accessed by the general public are known as which of the following?
    a. Commercial properties
    b. Private properties
    c. Public accommodations
    d. Special use properties

44. If you, as a broker, sell your own property, the difference between the cost of the property when you bought it and the amount you were able to sell it for is known as your:
    a. Principle
    b. Profit
    c. Prorate
    d. Plotting

45. As a broker, under which of the following agreements are you promised a commission, but only if you are the one to secure the buyer?
   a. Open listing
   b. Open house
   c. Exclusive right of sale
   d. Due on sale clause

46. Jason rents his apartment on January 9. The apartment rents for $850 a month. The landlord prorates the rent and only charges Jason for the days he will be renting the apartment (not including the start day). What will the prorated rent for the month be?
   a. $246.78
   b. $850.00
   c. $603.23
   d. $750.00

47. Michael is appraising a 100-year-old Victorian manor. The total livable square footage is 2,650. The one-car garage is 300 square feet. The estimated cost per square footage is $121 for the livable area and $60 for the garage. What is the reproduction cost new (RCN) for the property?
   a. $36,300
   b. $18,000
   c. $2,950
   d. $338,650

48. The senior class rents a beach house for 10 days in March for spring break. The beach house rents for $4,260 a month. The landlord prorates the rent and charges the group for only the days they will be renting the apartment, with a daily upcharge of 12% of the daily rent. What will the prorated rent for the 10 days be?

  a. $1,539
  b. $1,374
  c. $3,000
  d. $2,039

49. Bell is appraising a 200-year-old gothic castle. The total livable square footage is 18,620. The estimated cost per square footage is $250 for the livable area, adjusted for repairs and appreciation. What is the reproduction cost new (RCN) for the property?

  a. $4,655
  b. $4,655,000
  c. $465,500
  d. $4,650

50. A Manhattan loft rents for $460 a square foot with an index of 52.15. The index increases to 76.4. What is the adjustable rental rate?

  a. $824.90
  b. $326.80
  c. $673.90
  d. $690.30

51. Josiah has an estimated monthly housing expense of $2,020, and his monthly obligations total $3,475. If Josiah has a monthly gross income of $6,860, what is the total obligations ratio?

  a. 61%
  b. 21%
  c. 81%
  d. 51%

52. Emily has an estimated monthly business expense of $2,200, and her monthly obligations total $4,350. If Emily has a monthly gross income of $10,620, what is the total obligations ratio?
    a. 41%
    b. 31%
    c. 21%
    d. 12%

53. Travis is building a paddock on the side of his barn. The paddock is 45 feet wide and 75 feet long. What is the area of the paddock?
    a. 3,375 square feet
    b. 375 square feet
    c. 305 square feet
    d. 3,250 square feet

54. Buck purchased a 20-acre ranch with a down payment of $260,000 and a mortgage of $2,450,600 at an interest rate of 2% for a 30-year term. The monthly payments are $7,800. What is the loan-to-value ratio?
    a. 60%
    b. 30%
    c. 70%
    d. 90%

55. An art studio rents for $22 per square foot with an index of 0.22. The index increases to 0.32. What is the adjustable rental rate?
    a. $12
    b. $32
    c. $42
    d. $62

56. What does the National Priorities List qualify a contaminated property for?
    a. Assistance, cleanup and removal of hazardous waste
    b. Fines and penalties for the contamination of a site by hazardous materials
    c. The illegal use of hazardous materials in public venues
    d. The destruction of hazardous waste in an unsafe way

57. Through which of the following laws is the Internal Revenue Service permitted to collect taxes on properties that are sold and receive capital gain?
    a. Personal property tax law
    b. Federal income tax law
    c. Property gains law
    d. Sales tax law

58. As part of the federal income tax law, tax breaks on capital gains for a primary residence are offered to which of the following parties?
    a. Homeowners
    b. Corporations
    c. Partnerships
    d. Small business owners

59. Advantages to home ownership can include a deduction in the interest rate on a mortgage, property tax deductions and Internal Revenue Service withdrawal under which of the following provisions?
    a. Property Owners Association
    b. Green Belt Law
    c. Federal income tax law
    d. Search and Seizure Law

60. An IRA withdrawal can allow first-time homebuyers to make a withdrawal from an IRA account, tax-free, when it is used toward the down payment on a first home in an amount not more than:
    a. $250,000
    b. $100,000
    c. $75,000
    d. $10,000

61. Sales associates and brokers should check a list before making sales and solicitation calls to avoid federal penalties in the event that they call someone who is registered not to receive solicitation calls. This is covered under which of the following?
    a. Florida Do Not Call Law
    b. Fair Housing Act
    c. National Do Not Call Registry
    d. Florida Institutions Reform, Recovery, and Enforcement Act

62. To ensure that as a sales associate or broker, you are not breaking federal or state Do Not Call laws, you should do which of the following before making sales and solicitation calls?
    a. Check both the federal and state Do Not Call lists to ensure the individual you are calling is not on either one
    b. Ensure that the individual you will be calling is not on the National Do Not Call Registry
    c. Ensure that the individual you will be calling is not on the state Do Not Call list
    d. Make sales calls without additional information on the parties you are calling

63. In which of the following years was the National Do Not Call Registry established?
    a. 1983
    b. 1993
    c. 2003
    d. 2013

64. Which of the following organizations is responsible for establishing the National Do Not Call Registry?
    a. Federal Bureau of Investigation
    b. Federal Department of Homeland Security
    c. Federal Communications Commission
    d. Federal Secret Service

65. If you violate the National Do Not Call Registry, you may face fines not to exceed:
    a. $1,000
    b. $7,000
    c. $11,000
    d. $17,000

66. All of the following are exempt from the National Do Not Call Registry, except:
    a. Phone calls representing or regarding political matters
    b. Phone calls about or from charitable organizations
    c. Phone calls for the purpose of conducting surveys by telephone
    d. Phone calls from telemarketers regarding a product or service

67. Under the National Do Not Call Registry, you can be contacted by a business with which you have previously conducted business within the past ____ without penalty.

  a. 12 months
  b. 18 months
  c. 24 months
  d. 36 months

68. You can be contacted by a business or organization that you have submitted an application to for the limited time of __ days under the National Do Not Call Registry.

  a. 30
  b. 45
  c. 60
  d. 90

69. Under which federal law are financial agencies required to maintain and report mortgage information publicly?

  a. Home Mortgage Disclosure Act
  b. Fair Housing Act
  c. Interstate Land Sales Full Disclosure Act
  d. Both B and C

70. How is the information collected under the Home Mortgage Disclosure Act used in regard to communities?

  a. To show the amount of inventory that is being purchased in an area during a specific time frame
  b. To help show whether lenders are meeting the needs of their communities
  c. To compare the lender's interest rates in a given area
  d. To highlight undesirable areas that are not being purchased

71. Public officials and government bodies use information collected under the Home Mortgage Disclosure Act to highlight areas with which of the following problems?
    a. A buyer's market
    b. A seller's market
    c. Discrimination in lending
    d. High-interest rates

72. When using mortgage information under the Home Mortgage Disclosure Act, which of the following is done to protect borrowers?
    a. Share information with government officials and third-party solicitors
    b. Disclose a borrower's financial information, including credit reports and scores
    c. Poll the ethnicities that are buying a property in a given area
    d. Alter personal information to protect a borrower's identity

73. The capital gains exclusion, also known as the home sales tax exclusion, provides which of the following for homeowners who are selling their main or primary home and receiving a profit from that sale?
    a. Tax deduction on money earned from the sale of the property
    b. Tax credits for the purchase of new properties
    c. Higher taxes due to a large earning from the sale of the property
    d. Tax exemption on money earned from the sale of the property

74. Once any existing balance on a real estate mortgage has been brought to a zero balance, money earned after the sale of real estate is known as which of the following terms?
    a. Taxable income
    b. Capital gains
    c. Home equity
    d. Profit margin

75. Under the capital gains tax exclusion, single individuals may be allowed to exclude up to ______ for money earned on the sale of their home.

a. $100,000
b. $150,000
c. $250,000
d. $500,000

76. Under the capital gains tax exclusion, married couples may exclude up to ______ from profits earned on the sale of their home.

a. $250,000
b. $500,000
c. $750,000
d. $1,000,000

77. To qualify for tax exemption under the capital gains exclusion, the home that you are selling must be which of the following?

a. A vacation home
b. A rental property
c. An investment property
d. A primary home

78. You can qualify for a capital gains exclusion only every:

a. Year
b. 24 months
c. 5 years
d. 8 years

79. You are required to reside in a home for a minimum of ____ before you can qualify for a home sales tax exclusion.

   a. 2 years
   b. 3 years
   c. 5 years
   d. 8 years

80. If you have lived in a home for at least two years and ____, then you qualify for a home sales tax exclusion when you sell.

   a. It is an investment property you rent out but do not live in
   b. It is the property you own closest to work
   c. It is a vacation home close to your family
   d. It is your only home

81. What government agency regulates and manages the capital gains exclusion provisions?

   a. The Internal Revenue Service
   b. The county tax collector's office
   c. The state tax collector's office
   d. The Federal Reserve

82. The Mortgage Interest Deduction Act serves which of the following purposes?

   a. To provide a tax credit for mortgage interest that is due
   b. To provide a tax deduction on mortgage interest that has been paid
   c. To tax a new property for personal property taxes
   d. To pay off the interest of a mortgage with your taxes

83. What three requirements does a property need to meet in order to be classified as a home?
    a. Heat, city sewer, city water
    b. Amenities, acreage, attached physical structure
    c. Sleeping quarters, cooking facilities, toilet facilities
    d. Acreage, fenced yard, paved driveway

84. Under the mortgage interest deduction law, a home mortgage that is obtained during divorce proceedings can be eligible for a tax cut if the property owner had to do which of the following?
    a. Purchase a new home after a divorce
    b. Downsize to a smaller property
    c. Sell the house to liquidate the asset and divide it between the divorcing parties
    d. Buy out a spouse's portion of the home

85. As of what year are those who purchase a home allowed to use up to the first $750,000 in interest on any mortgage?
    a. 1997
    b. 2007
    c. 1987
    d. 2017

86. Which of the following federal laws is found under Title 12, Chapter 38 of the United States statutes?
    a. Federal tax deduction law
    b. Federal property owner law
    c. Federal foreclosure law
    d. Federal financing law

87. Which of the following provisions were made for homeowners as of January 2014 under federal foreclosure laws?
    a. Protection of homeowners during foreclosure proceedings
    b. Protection for lenders during foreclosure proceedings
    c. Restrictions for homeowners during foreclosure proceedings
    d. Increased power afforded to lenders during foreclosure proceedings

88. United States federal foreclosure laws are designed to help borrowers keep their property while working with lenders to:
    a. Create a mortgage buyout by the lender
    b. Create an alternative mortgage payment arrangement
    c. Assess the additional interest accrued for any non-payment
    d. Offer homeowners to go uncontested into the foreclosure process

89. In which of the following years was the Equal Credit Opportunity Act established?
    a. 1954
    b. 1964
    c. 1974
    d. 1984

90. Which of the following laws prohibits public assistance programs from denying an individual or group of individuals financial assistance based on race, religion, age, sex, marital status, sexual orientation or national origin?
    a. Fair Housing Act
    b. Real estate settlement procedures
    c. Capital gains exclusion
    d. Equal Credit Opportunity Act

91. The Consumer Credit Protection Act, also known as the Truth in Lending Act, requires lenders to provide borrowers with a clear disclosure of annual percentage rates associated with a loan how soon after receiving their application?

a. 24 hours
b. 3 days
c. 1 week
d. 30 days

92. The Truth in Lending Act is regulated by what federal organization?

a. Treasury Department
b. Secretary of State
c. Federal Reserve
d. Internal Revenue Service

93. All loans that are funded or associated with the federal government are protected under which of the following laws?

a. Truth in Lending Act
b. Mortgage Disclosure Act
c. Capital Gains Exclusion
d. Real Estate Settlement Procedures Act

94. Under the Real Estate Settlement Procedures Act, _____ are required to provide informational booklets and good faith estimates for closing costs.

a. Brokers
b. Lenders
c. Sales associates
d. Borrowers

95. The Real Estate Settlement Procedures Act was created by which of the following organizations?
    a. Financial Protection Bureau
    b. National Treasury
    c. Federal Bank of America
    d. Secretary of State

96. Under the Real Estate Settlement Procedures Act, lenders must provide borrowers with a closing disclosure a minimum of how many days before closing?
    a. 3 days
    b. 7 days
    c. 15 days
    d. 28 days

97. In what year was the Fraud Enforcement and Recovery Act established?
    a. 1989
    b. 1999
    c. 2009
    d. 2019

98. Who does the federal government allow to enforce laws against mortgage fraud under the Fraud Enforcement and Recovery Act?
    a. The Central Intelligence Agency
    b. Federal law enforcement officials
    c. The Federal Bureau of Investigation
    d. The Department of Homeland Security

99. What percentage of states have laws regarding mortgage fraud?

a. 33%
b. 48%
c. 62%
d. 74%

100. Those who are found guilty of violating the Fraud Enforcement and Recovery Act can be fined up to ____ and face up to ____ years in prison.

a. $1,000 and 13 years
b. $1,000,000 and 30 years
c. $100,000 and 3 years
d. $100,000,000 and 30 years

# Answers – Broker Practice Test 2

1. Answer: a. Interpleader
   When a broker has no financial claim in a legal matter, the broker is known as an interpleader.

2. Answer: b. Escrow disbursement order
   While the real estate commission issues a determination of who is entitled to disputed funds, funds must be held in a brokerage escrow account. The Florida Real Estate Commission must be informed within 10 business days if the dispute is settled. The settlement is an Escrow Disbursement Order.

3. Answer: c. Good faith doubt
   Good faith doubt is when a broker doubts the intentions of either party to act in good faith according to the contract.

4. Answer: b. Brokers negotiate their own commissions
   In the State of Florida, brokers negotiate their own commissions.

5. Answer: c. Broker
   Anyone who is a general partner, officer or director of a brokerage partnership or corporation is a broker.

6. Answer: c. Sole proprietorship
   If a broker is the only owner in a business, holds full liability for the business, retains an active broker's license, and has a business registered under either his/her own name or a trade name, this is a sole proprietorship.

7. Answer: a. Register as a real estate broker
   A sole proprietorship, general partnership, limited partnership, limited liability partnership, corporation and limited liability company are all business entities that may register as real estate brokers.

8. Answer: a. A real estate brokerage general partnership
   If you register as a partnership with the Department of Business and Professional Regulation and have at least one partner who is an active broker, this makes it a real estate brokerage general partnership.

9. Answer: b. Trade name
   When brokers use a business name that is separate from their personal legal name, they are using a trade name.

10. Answer: a. Through an electronic testing system
    You will take your Florida Real Estate Broker's exam on a computer at a Pearson VUE testing facility.

11. Answer: b. Exclusive listing agent
    When a property owner gives a broker the sole right to sell, the broker is the exclusive listing agent.

12. Answer: b. Personal assistant
    It is not uncommon for a broker to hire an individual to handle routine responsibilities such as answering phones, filing paperwork and scheduling appointments.

13. Answer: c. Policy manual
    To run a brokerage smoothly, brokers should have a formal policy manual.

14. Answer: a. Record-keeping
    Record-keeping includes maintaining monthly cash receipts, a disbursement journal, a master journal, a monthly reconciliation statement, individual customer ledger sheets and a master customer ledger.

15. Answer: d. Mediation
    Mediation is a non-binding process in which parties try to work out a legal matter with the help of a non-biased third party in order to avoid taking the matter before the courts.

16. Answer: c. Immediately
    The auditing agent will release the findings to the broker or brokerage immediately after the audit concludes.

17. Answer: c. 7
    The Florida Real Estate Commission has a seven-step disciplinary process. First, a complaint is made. Second, an investigation is conducted. Third, a probable cause panel is formed and the information is brought before it. Fourth, a formal complaint is made (if there is enough proof found in steps one and two). Fifth, either an informal conference or a formal hearing takes place. Sixth, the Florida Real Estate Commission issues its final order. And seventh, the real estate agent may then choose whether or not to appeal.

18. Answer: d. Comparative market analysis
    You will use a comparative market analysis to compare properties that are similar to the one you are trying to sell. You will look at locations, as well as similarity in size, rooms, square footage, and so on to help determine the market for the property you are preparing to list. You will also study

the amount of inventory similar to your property, the amount of demand for properties like yours and whether there are properties out there like yours that have remained on the market over the last year and just are not moving.

19. Answer: c. Appraisal values
Appraisal values can be made based on the investment value, assessed value, liquidation value, salvage value, insurable value and market value.

20. Answer: a. The appraisal process
A real estate agent must thoroughly explain the appraisal process to clients.

21. Answer: b. Sales comparison approach
To use the sales comparison approach, you will collect data on comparable properties, the adjustment of the comparable sales price and the reconciliation of the adjusted sales price.

22. Answer: c. Transactional characteristics
Transactional characteristics include determining the condition of a sale, making adjustments for the financing terms and making adjustments for market conditions.

23. Answer: b. 4 steps
There are four steps to the cost depreciation approach. Figure out the cost both to buy the property and reproduce it through new construction. Consider the amount of depreciation that has accrued through normal wear and tear, design faults and/or outside sources that affect the property. Compare the cost of similar properties, the value of your

property and the cost of improvements to your property. Use the depreciated value and the cost to improve to find the property value.

24. Answer: b. Comparables
Comparables are used when you conduct a comparative market analysis.

25. Answer: a. Building community relationships
The world of real estate is a business that relies heavily on the connections you make, the reputation you have, how well you perform and take care of those that you provide services to, and whether or not you leave clients with a good impression of you by the time you are done conducting business together.

26. Answer: c. Balance sheets and income statements
As a real estate agent, when you are conducting a business valuation, you have to have relevant, up-to-date information on that property. A property balance sheet and income statement will be among the most important documents for you to maintain records of.

27. Answer: d. Valuation approaches
Some of the ways you may use the approach to valuation system include determining the value of the comparable sales, cost appreciation value, income capitalization value and liquidation value.

28. Answer: a. Single agent notice
Brokers are legally required to provide clients and customers with a single agent notice any time they are acting in such a capacity during real estate transactions.

29. Answer: b. Dual agent
Dual agent is a title applied to a broker any time he/she acts as the agent for both parties in a real estate transaction.

30. Answer: c. Unauthorized practice of law
In the State of Florida, real estate agents are allowed to prepare sale and purchase contracts, listing agreements, buyer broker agreements and options contracts without violating the law.

31. Answer: a. Listing agreement
Clients often sign a listing agreement when a broker or brokerage is hired to sell a property. As part of that, the property owner must give the broker as much information about the property as possible. This includes but is not limited to title insurance documents, surveyor documents and mortgage documents. The more information you have on the property, the better equipped you will be to sell the property.

32. Answer: b. Lead-based paint
As a broker or sales associate, disclosing hazards of a property is a part of your job. In homes built before 1978, you will be required to provide a pamphlet from the Environmental Protection Agency (EPA) regarding possible home hazards.

33. Answer: d. Client evaluation
As a broker, you will have clients you serve for a variety of reasons. The service you will be providing for them will determine the amount and type of information you need to know about the person or party. To gain the information that you need to know, you may do a client evaluation. This can include financial statements, a list of assets, capital and losses, just to name a few.

34. Answer: b. Rent concession
Rent concession can occur both residentially and commercially. In some cases, landlords or brokers who are working as property managers will offer rent concessions to tenants as compensation for part or all of their rent, moving expenses or a lease buy. In other cases, a property manager or property owner may hire a maintenance person or property manager that will live on-site at a property. Upon being retained, and in addition to their hourly wage or salary, such individuals may also be offered a rental concession where they either pay a discounted portion of the typical rent or no rent at all as part of their employment package.

35. Answer: a. Three-day notice
When a tenant is in breach of a lease and has not paid rent, the broker acting as the property manager, a landlord or the property owner may issue a tenant with a three-day notice. The three-day notice requires the tenant to either rectify the situation or be out of the property within 72 hours of receiving the notice.

36. Answer: a. A variable lease
As a real estate broker, when you are managing rental properties and a tenant pays rent based on an index, this is known as a variable lease.

37. Answer: b. An upfront mortgage insurance premium
An upfront mortgage insurance premium is due when the property is being closed on, most commonly in FHA loans, and requires that the entire amount due for the insurance premium is paid up front and in one bulk payment.

38. Answer: c. A title
A title is a legal document that shows ownership of a property. In most cases, an individual receives a claim to the property when he/she owns

that property outright and there are no loans or lien left on it. Sometimes, when using a property as collateral, the title must be surrendered to the lender until the loan is paid off in full.

39. Answer: c. Sublease
The arrangement that Bill makes with Hannah is a sublease. Depending on the lease contract that a tenant is under, subleasing may not be permitted. Property managers should be very familiar with the leases they use and which properties under their management do or do not allow subleasing.

40. Answer: d. A property that is under appraisal or potentially going to be under contract
Subject property refers to a piece of real estate that is either under contract for an appraisal or potentially going to be entered into a contract to sell by the property owner.

41. Answer: b. A developer
Sales associates are not permitted to work without supervision, and their real estate transactions are done under the name of their supervisor or brokerage.

42. Answer: b. Real estate services
BAR SALE is an acronym for Buy, Appraise, Rent, Sell, Auction, Lease, Exchange.

43. Answer: c. Public accommodations
Public accommodations include hotels, motels, extended stay hotels and more.

44. Answer: b. Profit

If you, as a broker, sell your own property, the difference between the cost of the property when you bought it and the amount you were able to sell it for is known as your profit.

45. Answer: a. Open listing
    Your client hires you to secure a buyer to purchase their real estate property. You are under contract to get a commission, but only if you are the one to find the buyer because you and the client have an open listing agreement.

46. Answer: c. $603.23
    Jason will pay a prorated rent of $603.23.

47. Answer: d. $338, 650
    The reproduction cost new of the Victorian manor is $338,650.
    2650 x 121 + 300 x 60 = $338,650

48. Answer: a. $1,539
    The prorated rent for the beach house is $1,539.

49. Answer: b. $4,655,000
    The reproduction cost new for the gothic castle is 4,655,000.

50. Answer: c. $673.90
    The adjustable rental rate for the Manhattan loft is $673.90.

51. Answer: d. 51%
    The total obligations ratio is 51%.

52. Answer: a. 41%
The total obligations ratio is 41%.

53. Answer: a. 3,375 square feet
The total area of the paddock is 3,375 square feet.

54. Answer: d. 90%
The loan-to-value ratio for the ranch is 90%.

55. Answer: b. $32
The adjustable rental rate is $32.

56. Answer: a. Assistance, cleanup and removal of hazardous waste
The National Priorities List grants assistance and support, cleanup resources and hazardous waste removal to properties that warrant the services.

57. Answer: b. Federal income tax law
The IRS is permitted by federal income tax laws to collect taxes on properties when they are sold and when they receive capital gains through such sales.

58. Answer: a. Homeowners
As a part of federal income tax law, tax breaks offered on capital gains that are earned from the sale of a primary home benefit the homeowners and can help in their next venture.

59. Answer: c. Federal income tax law
Federal income tax laws offer a wide array of incentives to make homeownership enticing, such as lower interest rates on mortgages, property tax deductions, tax rebates and other similar advantages.

60. Answer: d. $10,000
An IRA withdrawal can allow first-time homebuyers to make a withdrawal from an IRA account, tax-free, when it is used toward the down payment of a first home in an amount not more than $10,000.

61. Answer: c. National Do Not Call Registry
Sales associates and brokers should check the National Do Not Call Registry before making sales and solicitation calls.

62. Answer: a. Check both the federal and state Do Not Call lists to ensure the individual you are calling is not on either one
All those in sales should consider the non-solicitation registries and lists when making calls. This especially pertains to sales associates and brokers.

63. Answer: c. 2003
The National Do Not Call Registry was enacted in 2003.

64. Answer: c. Federal Communications Commission
The National Do Not Call Registry was established by and is overseen and regulated by the Federal Communications Commission, also known by the acronym FCC.

65. Answer: c. $11,000
Those who violate the National Do Not Call Registry can face fines of up to but not exceeding $11,000.

66. Answer: d. Phone calls from telemarketers regarding a product or service
Exceptions to the National Do Not Call Registry include phone calls representing or regarding political matters; phone calls regarding charities, raising funds for charities, and sharing information about charitable organizations; and for the purpose of conducting surveys by phone. However, telemarketers are not protected by such an exclusion.

67. Answer: b. 18 months
After conducting business with an individual or entity, that company is allowed to solicit you with phone calls for no more than 18 months after your business together has concluded.

68. Answer: d. 90
Under the National Do Not Call Registry, businesses that you have submitted an application to are permitted to call you for the limited time of up until 90 days after the date on the application.

69. Answer: a. Home Mortgage Disclosure Act
Federal law requires financial agencies, under the terms of the Home Mortgage Disclosure Act, to be forthcoming and report their mortgage lending information.

70. Answer: b. To help show whether lenders are meeting the needs of their communities
The data collected under the Home Mortgage Disclosure Act is used in part to determine if lenders are meeting the needs of their communities.

71. Answer: c. Discrimination in lending
Information gathered under the Home Mortgage Disclosure Act is used by public officials and government bodies to determine if there is any discrimination in lending.

72. Answer: d. Alter personal information to protect a borrower's identity
Under Title 12: Banks and Banking, Chapter 11: Federal Home Loan Banks, a lender must alter the personal information of their borrowers in order to protect their identities when lenders disclose mortgage information.

73. Answer: a. Tax deduction on money earned from the sale of the property
The home sales tax exclusion, also known as the capital gains exclusion, provides tax deductions on a set dividend of money earned on the sale of a property.

74. Answer: b. Capital gains
Capital gains is the money that is earned after the sale of real estate once any mortgage loans still remain on the property are brought to a zero balance. Capital gains can also be referred to as a profit on a sale.

75. Answer: c. $250,000
A single individual will be allowed to exempt $250,000 under the capital gains exclusion if the individual sells his/her main home.

76. Answer: b. $500,000
The capital gains exclusion is a tax exemption that makes provisions for married couples by allowing the couple to have up to $500,000 tax-exempt from any capital gains.

77. Answer: d. A primary home
In order for a property to qualify for tax exemptions under the capital gains exclusion, the property is required to be the seller's primary home, with few exceptions.

78. Answer: b. 24 months
An individual can qualify for the capital gains exclusion once every 24 months, but only in the event that he/she meets the other requirements as well.

79. Answer: a. 2 years
You can qualify for the home sales tax exclusion if the home being sold is your primary home and you lived in that home for at least two years in a five-year period.

80. Answer: d. This is your only home
If the home you are selling is the only home you have and you have lived in the house for at least two years, then you qualify for the home sales tax exclusion when you sell.

81. Answer: a. The Internal Revenue Service
The Internal Revenue Service regulates and manages the capital gains exclusion provisions.

82. Answer: b. To provide a tax deduction on mortgage interest that has been paid
The Mortgage Interest Deduction Act provides a tax deduction on mortgage interest that has been paid on the property.

83. Answer: c. Sleeping quarters, cooking facilities, toilet facilities
In order to be classified as a home, the property must have designated sleeping quarters, cooking facilities and toilet facilities.

84. Answer: d. Buys out a spouse's portion of the home
United States mortgage interest deduction laws allow home mortgages that are obtained during divorce proceedings to be eligible for federal tax cuts if the property owner buys out a spouse's portion of the home.

85. Answer: d. 2017
As of 2017, those who purchase homes will be allowed to use the first $750,000 in interest on any mortgage.

86. Answer: c. Federal foreclosure law
Federal foreclosure laws can be found under Title 12: Banks and Banking, Chapter 38: Multifamily Mortgage Foreclosure and Chapter 38A: Single Family Mortgage Foreclosure of United States Code.

87. Answer: a. Protection of homeowners during foreclosure proceedings
The federal foreclosure laws enacted additional provisions in January 2014 to assist homeowners with certain protections during foreclosure proceedings.

88. Answer: b. Create an alternative mortgage payment arrangement
Federal foreclosure laws are designed to help borrowers keep their property while working with lenders to create alternative mortgage payment arrangements.

89. Answer: c. 1974
The Equal Credit Opportunity Act was established in 1974.

90. Answer: d. Equal Credit Opportunity Act
The Equal Credit Opportunity Act prohibits public assistance programs from denying an individual or group of individuals financial assistance based on race, religion, age, sex, marital status, sexual orientation or national origin.

91. Answer: b. 3 days
The Truth in Lending Act requires lenders to provide borrowers with a clear disclosure of annual percentage rates associated with a loan within three days of receiving their application.

92. Answer: c. Federal Reserve
The Federal Reserve regulates the provisions of the Truth in Lending Act.

93. Answer: d. Real Estate Settlement Procedures Act
All loans and funding provided by the United States government are protected under the Real Estate Settlement Procedures Act.

94. Answer: b. Lenders
Under the provisions of the Real Estate Settlement Procedures Act, lenders are responsible for furnishing information booklets and good faith estimates for closing costs to borrowers.

95. Answer: a. Financial Protection Bureau
The Financial Protection Bureau is responsible for the provisions and enforcements under the Real Estate Settlement Procedures Act.

96. Answer: a. 3 days
The Real Estate Settlement Procedures Act integrated closing disclosure laws requiring lenders to provide borrowers with a closing disclosure no less than three full days before closing.

97. Answer: c. 2009
The United States government enacted the Fraud Enforcement and Recovery Act in 2009.

98. Answer: b. Federal law enforcement officials
Under the Fraud Enforcement and Recovery Act, federal law enforcement officials may pursue individuals who commit mortgage fraud

99. Answer: a. 33%
33% of states have laws regarding mortgage fraud and more than 33% have provisional laws to protect their state residents.

100. Answer: b. $1,000,000 and 30 years
Those who violate the Fraud Enforcement and Recovery Act can be fined up to $1,000,000 and face up to 30 years in prison.

# References

1. **Florida Department of Business and Professional Regulation – DBPR**
   https://www.myfloridalicense.com/

2. **State of Florida.com**
   http://www.stateofflorida.com/real-estate-education/

3. **My Florida (The Official Page for the Sunshine State Government)**
   http://www.myflorida.com

4. **Pearson VUE**
   http://www.pearsonvue.com/fl/realestate

5. **Florida Department of Law Enforcement**
   http://www.fdle.state.fl.us/

Printed in Poland
by Amazon Fulfillment
Poland Sp. z o.o., Wrocław

68351738R00170